Van Morrison
in the 1970s

Peter Childs

sonicbondpublishing.com

Sonicbond Publishing Limited
www.sonicbondpublishing.co.uk
Email: info@sonicbondpublishing.co.uk

First Published in the United Kingdom 2022
First Published in the United States 2022

British Library Cataloguing in Publication Data:
A Catalogue record for this book is available from the British Library

Copyright Peter Childs 2022

ISBN 978-1-78952-241-9

The right of Peter Childs to be identified as the author of this work
has been asserted by him in accordance with the
Copyright, Designs and Patents Act 1988.

Typeset in ITC Garamond & ITC Avant Garde
Printed and bound in England

Graphic design and typesetting: Full Moon Media

DECADES | Van Morrison in the 1970s

Contents

'This is the place of my song-dream, the place the music played to me', whispered the rat, as if in a trance. 'Here, in this holy place, here if anywhere, surely we shall find Him!'.
'**The Piper at the Gates of Dawn**' from *The Wind in the Willows*.

In the Beginning: Astral Weeks

Astral Weeks (1968)

Personnel:
Van Morrison: acoustic guitar, vocals
Richard Davis: double bass
John Payne: flute, soprano saxophone ('Slim Slow Slider') (The flautist on 'Beside You' and 'Cyprus Avenue' is not credited)
Jay Berliner: classical and acoustic guitar
Connie Kay: drums
Warren Smith Jr.: vibraphone, drums, percussion
Barry Kornfeld: acoustic guitar ('The Way Young Lovers Do')
Larry Fallon: harpsichord ('Cyprus Avenue')
All songs by Van Morrison
Producer: Lewis Merenstein
Recorded at Century Sound, New York, September-October 1968
Release date: US: November 1968, UK: September 1969
Chart places: US: -, UK: 55 (2015)
Running time: 47:10
Tracklisting: Side One: 1. 'Astral Weeks', 2. 'Beside You', 3. 'Sweet Thing', 4. 'Cyprus Avenue'
Side Two: 1. 'The Way Young Lovers Do', 2. 'Madame George', 3. 'Ballerina', 4. 'Slim Slow Slider'

First and foremost, Van Morrison is a singer with a range of style and a depth of expression that places him among the great modern vocalists. He's also an accomplished musician and a consummate songwriter who'd cemented himself a place in music history by the age of 22. Born at the end of World War II – in August 1945 – he wrote and recorded at least three classic songs in advance of his musical rebirth with *Astral Weeks* in 1968. 'Gloria' – now a rock standard – was first recorded with Morrison's band Them, one of the most highly-regarded 1960s R&B groups. The song fast became a staple of garage rock, but is additionally famous for high-profile cover versions such as Jimi Hendrix's nine-minute 1968 rendition and Patti Smith's reworking on her 1975 debut album *Horses*. In its original version, where the recording is fired by primal energy and confident swagger, 'Gloria' is uproarious and elemental, making it as raw a slice of blue-eyed rock and soul as 'Louie, Louie', '(I Can't Get No) Satisfaction', or The Animals' version of 'The House Of The Rising Sun'.

Morrison's second classic – 'Brown Eyed Girl' – is listed among *Rolling Stone's* Top 500 Songs That Shaped Rock & Roll. It was his debut single as a solo artist, and went on to become one of the most requested and played songs on American radio. A sweet slice of summer-of-love pop with a 'sha-la-la' hook, it could've been recorded a dozen different ways, and took a long time to be crafted as a surefire hit. Too pop-flavoured for Morrison's taste at the time, the Bert Berns arranged and chart-oriented single was selected from over 20 takes, with Van rebelliously scatting in the fade. Backed by the sunshine harmonies of The Sweet Inspirations, it remains Morrison's best-known song.

The third, less well-known but foundational composition, was a blues song recorded in March 1967, with one of the darkest subjects imaginable: the fetid smell and claustrophobic feel of a girl's sickroom as she lies stricken with disease. Far from radio-friendly but inspired by a long tradition of songs about disease, including Jimmie Rodgers's 'T.B. Blues' (Rodgers died of tuberculosis), Morrison's ten-minute 'T.B. Sheets' is a portrait of hopelessness when someone is terminally ill. The lyric focuses on the singer – the patient's visitor – who is numbed by the sunlight shining through a crack in the windowpane, just wants to be free of the stale reek of the disease, needs the window opened to breathe, and above all aches to get out of the room. This is the strangest or saddest love song, told by someone who can't cope and just wants the tuberculosis sufferer placated: by a drink of water, the radio, another visitor, calming words. Addressed directly to the crying, bedridden Julie, the song is an inexorable haunting blues that has the smell of fear, helplessness, 'inadequacies', evasions and 'innuendos', as the numbing drums, bass, guitar and organ chug on minute-after-minute without release. This is punctuated by the shrieks of a pitiless harmonica and tambourine that could be the soundtrack to a funeral procession. It became the fitting signature song for Martin Scorsese's 1999 film *Bringing out the Dead* – the storyline of which follows a paramedic haunted by the patients he couldn't save. Morrison's long-time friend John Lee Hooker recorded a version on his 1972 album *Never Get out of these Blues Alive,* and the changed lyric in Hooker's version makes it even more pertinent to Scorsese's film, directly citing a hospital and a death wagon. Morrison himself duetted with Hooker on the album's title track.

These three fundamentally different songs hint at Morrison's eclecticism. They also reflect the breadth of his early musical influences. Elements of jazz, folk, country, soul, R&B, rock and classical weave throughout his 1970s output: the seminal decade of a long, distinguished solo career. He continues to make beautifully produced albums at a remarkable rate, with gems on each one. But the variety in his sound was most striking in the 1970s when each groundbreaking album was a new reputation-building addition to a still-small canon.

Morrison's father, George, bought imported American records and was especially enamoured with New Orleans jazz but had a wide music collection: Chicago blues, crooners, Country artists, and so on. In the 1950s – looking for a better life across the Atlantic like so many Irish migrants before him – George Morrison even travelled to Detroit, hoping to settle his family in the US. It didn't work out, but his ambition to see his family stateside was realised for a while in the 1970s after his son's success.

Meanwhile, that son – also named George – took to being known at school by the shortened form of his middle name Ivan. As a boy, Van was exposed to a prodigious range of music, and grew to love various jazz and blues singers and musicians, band leaders, gospel singers, and a whole spectrum of seminal performers, including Jimmie Rodgers, Sonny Terry and Brownie McGhee, Jimmy Reed, Frank Sinatra, Mahalia Jackson, Sonny Boy Williamson, Little Walter, Louis Prima, and especially Lead Belly. A wealth of music came to him through disparate sources, including Van's father's collection, a friend's brother's records, the few radio stations available, and the musical influence of family and older friends. Van's early interests led to his later love of R&B and of soul singers such as Sam Cooke, Solomon Burke, Bobby Bland and Ray Charles, not forgetting skiffle and Lonnie Donegan. Morrison told the *Irish Times* in 1998: 'The very first record I ever bought was 'Hootin' Blues' by Sonny Terry, and it cost 1/6d in Smithfield. I think the shop was called Smith's. There were rows and rows of records there'. He added that he bought his first guitar in Smithfield Market too.

Morrison also used to read his father's jazz books and devour stories about the Wild West, which would become another touchstone for his songs in the 1970s. From an early age, he visited Atlantic Records – Solly Lipsitz's shop in Belfast – every Saturday with his dad. In the *Irish Times* interview, Van explained:

Solly had all the records – Jazz and blues. Bo Diddley was on London American, and you could get his records in McBurney's (Premier Record Shop) in Smithfield. I loved Bill Haley, and I remember buying 'Razzle Dazzle'. And Gene Vincent and Jerry Lee Lewis – he had so

many good records one after another, and I bought his singles in
Smithfield. I still love Jerry Lee.

As recently as 2020, Morrison told *The Independent*: 'Solly was the
connection for all the recordings my father was into – mainly New Orleans
jazz like Sidney Bechet and Louis Armstrong's Hot Five, and Hot Seven
records. I used to pick out Lead Belly 78s. I sort of egged my father on to
buy those'. Highlighting an autobiographical touch on 'Astral Weeks', in
the late-1970s, Morrison told *Rolling Stone* that Huddie Ledbetter 'was my
guru. Somebody once sent me a huge poster of Lead Belly just beaming
down with a 12-string guitar. I framed it and put it up on the wall, and
I've had it on the wall everywhere I've been'.

Drawing particularly on jazz, Western music, blues, and also soul as
the secular version of gospel, Morrison's songwriting has remained
rooted in the sounds he heard in the late-1950s; in his early career he
predominantly employed the same song structures as in these records,
using chords he also found in the ballads and doo-wop songs of the
era. As a youth, he also developed a taste for country music, including
Hank Williams and the Carter family, with an appreciation of classical
music coming later. Van's mother was an amateur singer and through
community sing-alongs, Morrison was exposed to a whole raft of songs,
including traditional Irish ballads like 'The Star Of The County Down' and
other lyrics he later recorded with The Chieftains.

Violet Morrison additionally provided her son with an interest
in freethinking and spirituality. She took him to Jehovah's Witness
meetings a few times and his experience of the Kingdom Hall inspired
some aspects of his singing, with the venue itself becoming the subject
of the eponymous opening track on *Wavelength* (1978). In the song
'Summertime in England' on *Common One* (1980), Morrison mentions
the voice of 'Mahalia Jackson coming over the ether' and, like blues
and jazz, American gospel songs inspired the teenager, who began
experimenting with harmonica, guitar, and saxophone, but developed his
voice as a truly-defining instrument.

Morrison's songs are studded with references to his youth in East
Belfast, from his home on Hyndford Street, through locations in the local
area of Bloomfield, his school and the park in Orangefield, the railway
station near Cyprus Avenue, and the Hollow – mentioned in 'Brown Eyed
Girl' – where the Connswater river forms from the Knock and Loop rivers
on a stretch of water known locally as the Beechie.

Entering a music scene dominated by showbands, Morrison started off in the 1950s playing saxophone and singing in local bands. He went on to form a number of groups – most notably The Monarchs, with whom he toured Scotland, England and Germany, before success with Them in 1964. In London, on tour with the group, Morrison got to meet some of his heroes, including Little Walter and John Lee Hooker, who by coincidence, was staying at the same hotel. Morrison told Martin Chilton in 2020 in *The Independent:* 'When I came to London in the 1960s, Little Walter was staying at a hotel in Bloomsbury. Sometimes he would rehearse there in the afternoon, and the jam sessions I had with Little Walter, where I was just playing rhythm guitar for him, were brilliant'.

Van's group Them were named after the 1954 sci-fi/horror movie about giant mutant ants attacking civilization following an atomic-bomb test. The band are particularly revered for their famous residency at the Maritime Hotel in Belfast, with which they are forever associated in the same way that The Beatles are with The Cavern. After a couple of hit singles, Them were offered gigs in the United States. A two-month tour took the group to the West Coast on the back of the British invasion catalysed by The Beatles' 1964 success. By the time Them toured in May 1966, they'd already registered three hits – the traditional blues song 'Baby, Please Don't Go' (number 10 in the UK), whose B-side was 'Gloria'; 'Here Comes the Night' (2 in the UK; 24 in the US), and 'Mystic Eyes' (33 in the US). Of these three A-sides, only the last – partly inspired by watching an adaptation of *Great Expectations* on television – was written by Morrison. 'Here Comes the Night' – composed by one of Them's producers: the aforementioned Bert Berns – was also recorded in a slow and stately rendition by Lulu, which is worth comparing with Morrison's if only to appreciate the way Them's version ignites the song by (among other things) increasing the tempo and hammering home the chorus. Lulu's version was preferred by their shared label Decca as the single to release first but sold far less well than Them's did, charting only as high as number 50. Bowie's revamped cover on *Pin Ups* (1973), in many ways sought to emulate Them's version while revealing the difficulty of capturing the energy of the original hit: the emotional power of which Bowie had clearly fallen for.

On their US tour, Them played gigs with different support acts. Famously, at the Whisky a Go Go in Los Angeles they found themselves supported by the unsigned Doors, whose singer Jim Morrison duetted with his namesake on a version of 'Gloria'. It's a song the L.A. band continued to play live, with Jim displaying many of the moves he'd copied from Van. Poignantly, Morrison enlisted Doors drummer John Densmore to play on 'Gloria' for the Hollywood Bowl recording during the *Astral Weeks* tour that started in 2008.

Morrison first met future-wife Janet Rigsbee – who became known as Janet Planet – when Them moved to play San Francisco. The early relationship between the couple partly inspired aspects of several *Astral Weeks* songs, most notably 'Ballerina'. Concerts by Them also featured songs that later appeared on Morrison's live 1974 album with the Caledonia Soul Orchestra – *It's Too Late to Stop Now* – such as 'Help Me' and 'Ain't Nothin You Can Do'.

Morrison's Them built a strong US following on tour but folded soon afterwards amid managerial problems, pay disputes, and promotional issues with Decca Records. When his visa expired, Van flew back to London and then went home to Hyndford Street, where he saw out 1966 composing songs on a reel-to-reel tape recorder.

Now at a crossroads, Morrison continued to work on new material, including songs that surfaced in 1968, such as 'Astral Weeks'. Morrison told Donall Corvin in an interview in 1973 that he was waiting for a promised contract from Philips Records, which took 12 months to appear, by which time he had already heard from Bert Berns. Van had not only worked with Berns but respected him as the writer and producer of tracks like The Isley Brothers' 'Twist And Shout' and Solomon Burke's 'Everybody Needs Somebody To Love'. Berns invited Morrison to New York in March 1967 to record some tracks for his Bang Records label. When he went to the sessions, Morrison saw himself primarily as a vocalist, but Berns encouraged him to follow the singer-songwriter trend epitomised by Bang's rising star: ex-Brill-building hitmaker Neil Diamond.

Morrison has said he thought they were just making some singles, so from his perspective, several of the songs that were recorded were only ever intended as B-sides. However, Berns decided – without Morrison's knowledge – to release the eight songs as an album in September 1967, following the top ten success of 'Brown Eyed Girl' earlier that summer. Two further Morrison-written but typically Berns-sounding singles were released: 'Ro Ro Rosey', a love song for a teenage girl, with lyrics partly anticipating 'Cyprus Avenue', and the catchy 'Spanish Rose', sounding like a hybrid of 'Spanish Harlem' and 'Concrete And Clay'.

On the album, which was titled *Blowin' Your Mind!,* the tension is clear between Berns, who wanted a hit-friendly Latin-tinged pop production, and Morrison, who wanted to draw on his interest in the blues and different musical styles suited to an acoustic approach. Berns persuaded Morrison to cut more tracks in November 1967, including early versions of 'Beside You' and 'Madame George' that would surface in 1973 on the unauthorised album *T. B. Sheets* that Bang records released without Morrison's approval. The results were again unsatisfactory to Morrison, who was now more than concerned about his future working with Bert Berns.

Then, on 31 December 1967, Berns died of a heart attack. Rather than freeing Morrison of his contract with Bang, this put Van in a worse position. There was considerable ill feeling between Morrison and Berns' widow, who inherited the contract, and there were strong-arm business associates linked to organised crime who were interested in enforcing Morrison's contractual obligations to the record label. The singer was also harangued and threatened for the remainder of his time in New York, and this became one of the darkest periods in his life.

Van, Janet, and her son Peter moved to Cambridge, Massachusetts, where Morrison gigged around the local circuit, developing his set and honing songs that would appear on *Astral Weeks*. Key band recruits were local students John Payne (Harvard) on flute and Tom Kielbania (Berklee) on upright bass. They were joined for a while by Kielbania's college friend drummer Joey Bebo (Bebo has written a memoir of his experiences backing Morrison, suitably titled *In the Back of the Van*). The most notable gigs played were at the Catacombs close to the local college, and recordings made there of early versions of songs that later appeared on *Astral Weeks* have surfaced in recent years. The city's scene and Morrison's time there have been well-documented in Ryan H. Walsh's book *Astral Weeks: A Secret History of 1968*.

Warner Bros. eventually negotiated a get-out deal with Bang for Morrison. The costly severance arrangement included a commitment that Van's next batch of songs would be given to Bang, in addition to a share of profits from any singles released. Morrison was bitter for decades over the bad treatment he'd received, which included an attempt to deport him from the country that meant he had to marry if he wanted to stay in the US.

So, free from his original Bang contract, Morrison was still required to make recordings for the label as part of the get-out deal agreed by Warners. However, the publishing rights to Morrison's new music that Bang had negotiated proved to be of questionable value when the singer turned in a series of short off-the-cuff pieces of derisory musical nonsense to fulfil his obligations. The whole fiasco also led to a slew of repackaged copycat albums over the years, touting the New York sessions and their perfunctory offcuts as new or classic material. Morrison's bitterness towards the industry and artistic exploitation stems from all his early contracts, but especially this period, surfacing in the lyrics of many of his songs across the decades. It is finally worth noting that the legacy of the severance agreement with Bang even affected *Astral Weeks* because of another clause stipulating that two songs contracted to Bang had to appear on Morrison's first album with Warners. This provided an incentive to include newly recorded versions of 'Beside You' and 'Madame George'.

Having signed their new artist, Warner Bros. sent recording engineer and producer Lewis Merenstein to Ace Studios in Boston to check out Morrison's music. Though several previous Warner emissaries had left feeling uninspired, Merenstein was mesmerised by Morrison's acoustic material, such as 'Astral Weeks', so different from the Berns recording of 'Brown Eyed Girl'. He soon had quite specific ideas for how to present Van's unreleased songs and discussed reference points with Morrison, who, of course, had his own ideas. Partly to minimise studio time and partly to bring out the jazz mood, Merenstein and manager Bob Schwaid hired some of the best session musicians available. First and most influential was in-demand upright-bass player Richard Davis, who'd worked with many luminaries, including Miles Davis. Then there was revered drummer Connie Kay from the Modern Jazz Quartet who had also played on tracks like Big Joe Turner's seminal 'Shake, Rattle And Roll' (1954). The core players were completed by percussionist Warren Smith Jr., and guitarist Jay Berliner, who'd recorded with Charles Mingus and Harry Belafonte. Payne and Kielbania were considered surplus to requirements but still asked to hang around the studio to show the jazz players how the songs had been performed in Boston. Payne worked his way on to the record through sheer persistence, and at the end of the first day's recording was finally allowed to play flute on the one take of 'Astral Weeks'. Payne then played on later tracks: taking over from the anonymous session flautist. But Kielbania was never going to usurp his musical hero Richard Davis.

Astral Weeks was largely recorded live like a Blue Note jazz LP might have been. It took just three sessions – the unrehearsed free-jazz players following Morrison's lead, as he'd already lived and worked with most of the material for a long time. As an album, *Astral Weeks* sounds akin to a series of tone poems. Morrison has said he had an opera in mind at one stage and has described the songs as visual sketches. In line with this, the eight tracks seem to be contemplations, snapshots or epiphanies. We can think of the lyrics as fragmentary stories containing reveries connecting separated people and places through imagined out-of-body experiences. The words combine images and phrases from Morrison's present and past, blending geography and memory, astral projections and visualisations he'd later come to see in terms of Blakean visions. A musical antecedent would be Michael Considine's 19th-century ballad 'Spancil Hill' – about boarding a vision and flying home upon it to Erin's Isle from his new home in California.

The album's division into two halves – 'In the Beginning' and 'Afterwards' – was producer Merenstein's decision, as was the song order. A few other recordings were made – a song about Jesse James, another called 'Royalty', and a version of 'I've Been Working'. Most significant, however, was an inspired slow blues called 'Train' or 'Train, Train' that Morrison had been playing at gigs in Boston, and which features lyrics from the free-verse poem that adorns the album's back cover. Merenstein also edited down some of the recordings –notably cutting a section from the final song 'Slim Slow Slider', to make what he thought was a suitable finale to these tales of innocence and experience. Morrison has said that the songs, together with others not recorded, do have a story arc, but Merenstein altered the sequence, and the featured songs are only a subset of those in the overall conception. It's noticeable on the 2008/2009 *Astral Weeks* tour that Morrison performed the songs in a different sequence – moving 'Slim Slow Slider' back to follow 'Beside You', and placing 'The Way Young Lovers Do' immediately after 'Sweet Thing'. On the *Astral Weeks: Live at the Hollywood Bowl* recording, 'Astral Weeks' is supplemented by a song fragment called 'I Believe I've Transcended', which links the idea of a transcendent 'heaven' with Caledonia, and seemingly describes taking a child on a journey high above the valleys and mountains, to look down on the city. This fits with the imagery of the second song 'Beside You', where the singer takes a child on a journey gliding across the hills and mountains. The title 'I Believe I've Transcended' is repeated in the closing phrase of 'Autumn Song' from the 1973 album *Hard Nose the Highway*, which shares with 'Beside You' the invocation to turn around. In all, four of the *Astral Weeks: Live at the Hollywood Bowl* songs have short supplements – whether for artistic or other reasons – but each uses phrases familiar from Morrison's catalogue.

The 2008/2009 shows, which appended different song codas to the *Astral Weeks* originals, also feature Jay Berliner from the 1968 recording, and Morrison had hoped to have Richard Davis there too. Berliner even appears on Morrison's *Three Chords and the Truth* (2019), over fifty years after *Astral Weeks*.

The title 'Astral Weeks' appears to have been suggested by a visit Morrison made to his Belfast friend, artist and musician Cecil McCartney (whose acoustic album *Om* also came out in 1968). McCartney showed the singer some of his paintings on the subject of astral projection at a time when Van was working on the untitled song. The word 'astral' doesn't appear in the song, though the lyric refers to a home on high and a place way up in heaven.

The start of the lyrics to 'Astral Weeks' arguably implies how to understand the whole song cycle – as a series of excursions into a maze-like dreamscape – the singer putting the wheels of thought into motion, transported between visions, pushing at doors of perception, travelling in the mind's slipstreams. Combined with the title, the lyric suggests an astral projection from Belfast to San Francisco – most easily pictured as being from Morrison's bedroom with its Ledbetter posters, to Janet and her son's home on the far side of the ocean. Other songs speak of dreams, trances and visions, with most suggesting an out-of-body experience of some kind, transported by love, longing, ecstasy and the promise of escape – themes also present in James Joyce's *A Portrait of the Artist as a Young Man* with its closing invocation to the ancient artificer Daedalus to provide wings on which to fly, allowing the artist to break free from earthly limitations. The question 'Astral Weeks' ultimately poses, however, is about the possibility of finding connection: will the flight into the dream maze lead to the beloved? The quest for something that perhaps cannot be found is an idea Morrison's music would continue to express over the rest of the decade.

At the recording sessions, the production team consisted of Merenstein at the helm, alongside engineer Brooks Arthur and arranger Larry Fallon. According to Sean O'Hagan's *Guardian* article on *Astral Weeks* in 2008, Richard Davis said, 'We just listened to his songs one time, and then we started playing'. The four songs 'Madame George', 'Cyprus Avenue', 'Beside You' and the late addition 'Astral Weeks' were recorded in September on the first of the three days in the studio as the players instinctively took their instruments where the music and Morrison wanted to go. In October, the available players gathered again on two dates, recording more songs, some of which didn't make the album (largely because they didn't fit the mood envisaged by either Morrison or Merenstein). Fallon came up with arrangements (horns were added at Century Sound, and strings at Master Sound), including the harpsichord part he played on 'Cyprus Avenue'. Fallon had been the arranger on Nico's *Chelsea Girl* the year before, and later worked extensively with artists including Jimmy Cliff, Traffic and Mama Cass, also producing Richard Davis' 1971 album *The Philosophy of the Spiritual*.

Merenstein said he and Morrison discussed how to achieve a sound like jazz vibraphonist Bobby Hutcherson's song 'Tranquillity'. This was achieved on the second track, 'Beside You', albeit with the addition of Jay Berliner's plaintive Spanish guitar-playing. The song continues images and themes from 'Astral Weeks', such as the 'silence easy', with the singer accompanying a child on a transcendent journey, encountering ecstatic transformation in flight. 'Beside You' seems to tell of a twilight escape – little Jimmy heading out just before the 'Sunday six-bells chime', on the streets, roads, highways pointed to by the talismanic Broken Arrow (Neil Young's 'Broken Arrow' was recorded the year before for the 1967 *Buffalo Springfield Again* album). The 'six-bells' refers to St. Donard's Church in Bloomfield, where Morrison's parents married on Christmas Day 1941. The Church is at the crossroads of the Bloomfield Road and the Beersbridge Road, where Van's primary school was situated and off-which runs Cyprus Avenue. Other childhood memories are referenced elsewhere in Morrison's catalogue, most obviously in the song 'On Hyndford Street' from the 1991 album *Hymns to the Silence*. Earlier versions of 'Beside You' recorded with Berns and released in 1973 on *T.B. Sheets* and 1991 on *Bang Masters*, make a clearer Belfast connection through reference to the Northbridge railroad: suggesting the North Road railway bridge near Morrison's childhood home.

'Sweet Thing' – a love ballad of promises and predictions, taken from the October recordings – is the only side-one track featuring American jazz drummer Connie Kay. In the album sequence, the opening line draws its key image of the merry way from the previous track. However, the new song's most resonant link to 'Beside You' is the threefold repetition of 'never' and an echo of the earlier song's instruction to not wonder why things have to be. This third track is again about connection, and more clearly about lovers now: two people finding transcendence together. Other 'Sweet Thing' lyric elements recur on later albums, as the song provides repeated images of natural highs. Its seminal lines refer to gardens, which in Morrison's musical world are usually rain-wet – possibly the most quintessential image in his writing – suggesting an almost Edenic cleansing of the body and mind. The image recurs in the wet fields of the first line of 'The Way Young Lovers Do'.

After the singer drives a chariot down the streets in 'Sweet Thing', a carriage brings his lady from the fair along 'Cyprus Avenue': another ecstatic love song. However, the epiphany in 'Cyprus Avenue' contrasts with the feeling of transported joy throughout 'Sweet Thing'. Here, Morrison stews in a car seat, watching the girls walk by, frustrated by his inability to compose himself; tongue-tied, shaking like the autumn leaves on the trees, and all shook up inside like Elvis in 1957. When thinking about going to drink his cherry wine by the railroad that runs parallel, Morrison has a vision of his beloved coming towards him. The image may come from his country music hero Jimmie Rodgers and the moment in 'Blue Yodel No. 1' when the Singing Brakeman is going to 'where the water drinks like cherry wine'. Similarly, the image of the lonesome pining engine drivers would seem to be a nod towards the long tradition of Western train songs like Rodgers' 'Train Whistle Blues' (about a lonesome railroad train a-yonder coming down the track) and The Carter Family's 'Lonesome Pine Special'. Among countless potential reference points, there's also a studio outtake from the August-1972 *Hard Nose the Highway* sessions of Morrison singing Roy Acuff's 'Streamlined Cannon Ball': another song with a rail engineer and the sound of a lonesome train whistle. This is additionally a song in the spirit of Hank Williams' 'Mansion On The Hill', and Morrison is now up on the avenue with the same transported sense of heightened emotion that took him way up to Heaven in 'Astral Weeks'. 'Cyprus Avenue', for all its precise Belfast location, is no less ecstatic than 'Astral Weeks', but here the singer is 'caught' and 'conquered'. While he's trembling and transfixed, his love is triumphant in her 'revelation' – to use the term from live versions of the song in the 1970s: queen of the fair bedecked in ribbons in her horse-drawn carriage. This courtly image matches the chamber-music setting, with Larry Fallon's baroque harpsichord prominent throughout. The lady is in fact a schoolgirl walking down the avenue as the sun breaks through the trees – 14 years old: the age Morrison was when he left school for the last time, before turning 15 on the last day of August 1960. While there's no need for a mythical context, his revelation can also be considered in terms of the poetic genre of an aisling ('vision' or 'dream' poem) in which Ireland appears in personified female form – often young and bold.

Driven by Davis' fast-fingered bass-playing and Fallon's horn arrangement, 'The Way Young Lovers Do' is the album's fastest song, with its 6/8 time signature and jazz lineage from Coltrane's version of 'My Favourite Things'. Introduced by Smith's vibraphone and an acoustic guitar, it's the only track here to use Barry Kornfeld (as Jay Berliner was unavailable; in general, the dates had to work around the jazz musicians' schedules). After these gentle few seconds, the vocals, drums and bass dominate most of the opening, the strings and horns then all but drowning out Payne's flute. Following the love fool's autumn of 'Cyprus Avenue', in Merenstein's conception of the story arc, this up-tempo track ushers in the album's 'Afterwards' second side, in summertime (The sequence is reversed on the Hollywood Bowl recording). Not lyrically dissimilar to 'Moondance', it is the record's lightest, simplest track, and again there's the sunshine, the rain-wet fields, lovers kissing, dreaming, and dancing.

The album's other centrepiece – and for many, Morrison's masterpiece – is 'Madame George'. While he sings the name as 'Joy', he renamed the character George for the title, encouraging those readings of the song that emphasise the allusion to drag – suggesting the song's a goodbye letter to a transvestite madam, even though it appears as so much more: a farewell to a whole scene and an entire country. Morrison's early songs certainly have other references to queer culture (cf. 'He Ain't Give You None' and his live version of Bob Dylan's 'Just Like A Woman'). The 2014 publication *Lit Up Inside: Selected Lyrics* (edited by Eamonn Hughes) creates an official version of the words at least, and here dominoes are played 'in drag', even though Morrison once claimed it to be that dominoes is 'a drag'. The printed lyric also unexpectedly gives a gender symmetry in the shift from a 'she' jumping up and speaking, to a 'he' a few verses later. Without suggesting a direct influence, in the context of its Irish setting and its reference to Dublin, the story again is reminiscent of Joyce's farewell to his younger self in *A Portrait of the Artist as a Young Man*, and also of Stephen Dedalus' experience in the brothel scenes of Nighttown in the Circe chapter of *Ulysses*. Morrison says the song is not about one person but a spiritual feeling: emotions that arrive on the cool night air like, as the lyrics suggest, Guerlain's perfume Shalimar. Set in Belfast – not up but down on Cyprus Avenue – it's an adult's assembly of childhood images, such as collecting the tops off bottles, playing games, and throwing coins into the River Boyne as the train returns from Dublin to Belfast. Judging by its title alone, 'Madame George' appears to many people to be an elegy for its central character – a bohemian figure who may also be a seducer of boys in an atmosphere fuelled by wine and music. The scene is one of laughing and dancing, with cigarettes and objects that have to be dropped out into the street if the police arrive, reminiscent of the children casting pennies out the train window. Judging by the overall album, the song is very much one about the singer having to leave; having to say goodbye to Madame George in the backstreet like on 'Beside You', to catch a train away from the past. He is perhaps even going home on the back roads of 'Astral Weeks' to be reborn. But the string section's swirling ascension provides a nostalgic feeling of lost innocence.

Morrison refers to the writing of both 'Madame George' and 'Cyprus Avenue' as being stream-of-consciousness, yet his choice of his own first name George, and that of his father, in the title, seems unlikely to be completely unconscious. If we do see it as psychography or free writing, then the name George might also have been on his mind because of another female George. The wife of the poet W. B. Yeats – Georgie Hyde-Lees – was a major proponent of 'automatic script', which Yeats wrote about in his philosophy book *A Vision*. Taking against the name Georgie, Yeats called his wife 'George'. She died in August 1968, only weeks before the *Astral Weeks* recordings took place. In 2007, critic Tom Nolan argued in the *Wall Street Journal* that there was a connection between Hyde-Lees and the song.

As mentioned above, the earlier Bang version of 'Madame George' recorded in 1967 was released on the 1973 *T.B. Sheets* album, and featured a party atmosphere accompanying a lyric that differs in small but significant ways. In the earlier version of the song, it's unclear who has to go and catch a train, but the liner notes of the 1991 *Bang Masters* album nonetheless decide to explain the story thus:

'Madame George' is a song about saying goodbye to one's youthful friends and the old scene. It's a song about outgrowing a place and moving on. The lyric describes a party full of laughing, rowdy people. The singer – who finds himself no longer feeling like one of the gang – looks around for the last time, and then slips out into the night to catch a train that will take him away. As he moves toward the station, he hears the party growing softer behind him...

The melancholy of the *Astral Weeks* version is not present on this recording. Instead, Bert Berns' recording is faster and shorter. There's little sense of interior monologue, and the beautiful string section is, of course, also absent. A raucous studio atmosphere like on Dylan's 'Rainy Day Women #12 & 35' pervades the song to emphasise the party setting rather than the singer's emotions. Additionally, there's an extra set of four lines about losing self-control, being up against the bathroom door, the lights dimming and then 'touching him' in the front room. In other words, the sexual imagery is far stronger – there's a sense of 'you' indulging in foreplay, and the different musical arrangement changes the mood entirely. Another notable aspect to 'Madame George' is the second-person address, involving the listener in the way John Lennon does explicitly in parts of 'Lucy In The Sky With Diamonds'. Morrison appears to be singing either about himself or a universal 'you' (similar to – for example – Al Stewart on 'Year Of The Cat'), whereas the 'you' in every other song on *Astral Weeks* is a beloved. This device, though not important in itself, is arguably a key part of the appeal of 'Madame George'. Other song lyrics from the Bert Berns *Bang Masters* (e.g. 'The Back Room') have further echoes of the party scene of the 1967 'Madame George', but more importantly, have phrases (like 'cherry wine' and 'little girls coming home from school') that resurface on the *Astral Weeks* songs: providing a context for the evolution of the classic record.

When touring *Astral Weeks* in 2008/2009, Van's recreation closed with 'Madame George' and all its goodbyes, suggesting less a division between the 'In the Beginning' and 'Afterwards' album sides, than a song cycle about recreating the past as a way of understanding a journey to the present: as Dickens does in *Great Expectations*. However, in Merenstein's album sequence, 'Madame George' precedes two closing songs, creating a different narrative trajectory.

'Ballerina' and 'Madame George' share a key line about falling, the repeated refrain of which ends the *T.B. Sheets* version of 'Madame George'. Morrison has said the origin of the lyrics for 'Ballerina' lay in an image of an actress in an opera house ballet that flashed through his mind on his first visit to San Francisco. Its plea for the ballerina to fly into the arms of the singer may well again be a proposal to connect across continents. Like 'Astral Weeks', it speaks of entering into another's dreams, but now the singer forgets to slip into the other's sleep. Once more, he asks the 'child' to fly high and travel to him. Like 'Astral Weeks' he's waiting at the door, and like 'Cyprus Avenue', the protagonist is again tongue-tied and mumbling. About one minute was cut from 'Ballerina' on the original album, but the long eight-minute version was included as a bonus on the *Astral Weeks* 2015 edition. As far as is known, 'Ballerina' was probably, in fact, started in 1966 in Notting Hill, and revisited later that year in the States after Morrison met Janet Planet. It's likely to be the earliest-written of the tracks on the album, though The Doors' John Densmore – who has written about Morrison in his books *Riders on the Storm* and *The Seekers* – claims to have heard other songs from *Astral Weeks* in 1966, and Morrison *did* rewrite several of them over and over. Them even performed 'Ballerina' in Hawaii. Interestingly, 'Ballerina' is the only side two song to feature Berliner, as Kornfeld subs on the first track and Morrison plays acoustic guitar on 'Slim Slow Slider', while Berliner was so busy rushing between bookings at the time, that he arrived too late to the opening September session to appear on 'Madame George' (or 'Cyprus Avenue'). Davis is the one constant beside Morrison on all the tracks.

Introduced by one of the album's many inspired bass lines from Davis, 'Slim Slow Slider' was recorded in one take, though, according to Payne, the players thought it was a soundcheck. The song had been attempted with the full band, but it was decided to try it with just Morrison, bass, and saxophone. No strings were overdubbed. Merenstein placed an edit about two-thirds of the way through, where there's a short pause. On the full version (released on the album's 2015 remastered and expanded issue), the three players are heard to carry on improvising and Morrison sings the traditional hymnal line 'Glory be to him' over and over (as in 19th-century Scottish hymnist Hoaratius Bonar's 'Glory Be To Him Who Loved Us'). A connection to 'Ballerina' appears in the image of a girl about to fall, but the descent has reached a nadir for the beloved in 'Slim Slow Slider'. Once more, the speaker can't work out what to say or do. The reference to Ladbroke Grove suggests Morrison is back in Notting Hill, where Them's 'Friday's Child' and solo material like 'He Ain't Give You None' are set. As the final song on side two, 'Slim Slow Slider' unnervingly parallels side one's closing track. The singer is not watching his love walking down Cyprus Avenue but is equally helpless as he sees an *ex*-love walking down Ladbroke Grove. This is not a queen coming from the fair, but another girl who is dying, either metaphorically or literally. The song title itself is enigmatic but suggests someone in a slow decline, sliding away to death, or fatally sliding along lines of cocaine. Unlike the celebratory white horses on 'Cyprus Avenue', here we have the horse as an image of death – like the Bible's pale rider and the white horses taking his 'baby' to the burying ground in John Lee Hooker's 'Church Bell Tone', or the funerary symbol of the Celtic horse goddess Epona riding a white mare and accompanying the souls of the dead to the underworld. In the end, the lyric has intriguing imagery but is just a simple story of lost love – conjuring a very different mood but channelling the same experience of seeing his ex with another boy, as Morrison sang about on Bert Berns' 'Here Comes The Night'. The instrumentation is sparse, and foregrounds Payne's beautiful soprano saxophone. It's easy to take the song as a downbeat ending with the singer in great pain (as the classic 1979 Lester Bangs essay on 'Astral Weeks' interprets the album), or as at least uncomfortably numb as in 'T.B. Sheets'. Yet, as the closing track, it also points the listener back to 'Astral Weeks' and the quest to be born again. This fits with the lines that were removed – Morrison's incantation to God, like the words from the hymn 'Glory Be To God The Father'. These religious words might seem odd if it weren't for the references to heaven in 'Astral Weeks', suggesting that this praiseful chant is calling for death to bring a rebirth in Heaven: 'Glory be to him whose power, working in us, can do infinitely more than we can ask or imagine' (Ephesians 3:20). If an Irish precursor is sought, Joyce again provides the example of 'The Dead', which closes *Dubliners* with symbols and images of Christian and pagan rebirth in another story cycle.

The sound of *Astral Weeks* owes a debt to its producer Merenstein. Morrison would certainly have done it differently, and it would be fascinating to hear that alternative version (the 2009 live album is not it). What we have from the 1968 sessions is a one-off recording of a song suite connected through shared imagery and sound to create an ethereal musical scrapbook. In its particularity, the album, rather than the songs, is the product of two beautiful visions: Morrison's and Merenstein's. The tension between them may be said to have created one of the greatest recordings of the 20th century, but every one of the songs was a Morrison original, inspiring the alchemy of performance, production and sound; of musicians, arrangements and instrumentation.

Surfacing towards the end of November 1968, *Astral Weeks* wasn't in step with other mainstream rock albums released that year, such as *The Beatles*, *Music from Big Pink*, *Electric Ladyland* or *Beggar's Banquet*. But if we want parallels, it appeared very shortly after the debut solo album by another 23-year-old with a notable heritage in a successful 1960s band. Neil Young's self-titled debut LP is also bathed in string arrangements and was also a flop on its first release (on Young's birthday, 12 November 1968), leaving its creator despairing of studio interference.

Critic Greil Marcus has said that as an artist, Young is probably the best 'analogy' for Morrison. But perhaps the closest contemporary comparison for Morrison's 1968 record would be Nick Drake's *Five Leaves Left* – its recording begun before *Astral Weeks* when Drake had just turned 20, though it was released the following year. For many fans who cherish Morrison's album, these could now seem to be contemporary touchstones, if any are admitted, but its creator would look elsewhere. The obvious truth is that *Astral Weeks* isn't like any other album. Gestated over a few years, recorded in a few days, it was too unusual to gain wide recognition, taking reviews by Greil Marcus and Lester Bangs to bring it into the limelight.

Warner Bros. were also initially nonplussed by their new artist's different sound. With scant promotion and limited sales, the album was greeted with little fanfare; its singular quality communicated by a critical groundswell and the recommendations of listeners over the years. Disc jockey David Jensen perhaps best summed up its unique status when he observed that other records complement a mood, but *Astral Weeks* creates one. The 'sameness' and the string additions that Morrison would've avoided had he had full control in 1968 mean the eight songs coalesce into a musical reverie, and the lyric images work subliminally to draw the listener into a beguiling series of elusive short stories.

Boasting a contemplative and introspective cover photo by Joel Brodsky – who'd shot the covers of the first two Doors albums – *Astral Weeks* established several of the themes of Morrison's 1970s work: childhood visions, transformation, and transcendent experience. But the album was also unique. *Astral Weeks* was not radio-friendly, it bore no relation to his debut solo album, and its reference points were on the wrong side of the Atlantic for an American audience. For a struggling artist like Morrison, it was simply clear that the record was not a commercial success, yet he was tied to Merenstein's Inherit Productions company, for whom he had to do another album.

Sessions at Warner Bros. in the autumn ran through future cuts like 'When The Evening Sun Goes Down', 'Wild Night', 'Domino', and 'I Need Your Kind Of Loving', which finally appeared in a new version as the final track on 1991's *Hymns to the Silence*. Other simple acoustic demos were recorded – like the song 'Mona, Mona' with a 'Take Five' rhythm and basic repetitive lyrics about letting a cowboy ride, which finally surfaced on *Wavelength*'s 'Beautiful Obsession'. But these Warner sessions tracks – including the six-minute plea to come out and play tonight 'Bayou Girl' – were never fully worked up to see the light of day. Another unreleased and seemingly lost song – 'The Sky Is Full Of Pipers' – was cut in December with Berliner, Warren Smith Jr., Kielbania, and Barry Saltzman on drums, but *Astral Weeks* remained without a follow-up single. Morrison was left with the sense his career had been hijacked once more. He was broke and in need of a hit record, so making another *Astral Weeks* would not have seemed an attractive option. But a follow-up LP might've been Merenstein's aim, and other new songs that remain unreleased were demoed in the first half of 1969 – which we'll talk about in the run-up to *Moondance* and which suggest some work towards just such a possible sequel.

For Morrison, the music needed to be different, if just as good. He continued to rehearse with his Boston players Kielbania and Payne in New York at Merenstein's offices, and some promotional gigs further afield were arranged for early 1969, including the Avalon Ballroom in San Francisco. This was the first time Morrison had played outside New York or Massachusetts since 1967. But success seemed a long way away. Live work wasn't easy to come by, and gigs didn't always pay. Payne became frustrated and left around the end of 1968 before things started to look up. This happened when one of Payne's successors – the British-born Graham 'Monk' Blackburn – encouraged Morrison to move to Woodstock in search of a brand new start.

1970: Moondance and His Band and the Street Choir

Moondance (1970)

Personnel:

Van Morrison: rhythm guitar, tambourine, vocals

John Platania: lead and rhythm guitar

Jack Schroer: alto and soprano saxophone

Guy Masson: congas ('Come Running')

John Klingberg: bass

Jef Labes: organ, 'clavinette', piano

Gary Mallaber: percussion, drums, vibraphone

Collin Tilton: flute, tenor saxophone

Jackie Verdell, Emily 'Cissy' Houston, Judy Clay: backing vocals ('Crazy Love', 'Brand New Day')

Producer: Van Morrison

All songs by Van Morrison

Recorded at A&R Studios New York, August-September 1969

Release date: US: February 1970, UK: March 1970

Chart places: US: 29, UK: 32

Running time: 39:16

Tracklisting: Side One: 1. 'And It Stoned Me', 2. 'Moondance', 3.'Crazy Love', 4. 'Caravan', 5. 'Into The Mystic'. Side Two: 1. 'Come Running', 2. 'These Dreams Of You', 3. 'Brand New Day', 4. 'Everyone', 5. 'Glad Tidings'

In February 1969, Morrison relocated to a new rented home set into the Catskills cliffs on Oyaho mountain beside Woodstock – on Spencer Road: just down from Bob Dylan's house. The owner was Sid Bernstein: a friend of Lewis Merenstein. Morrison took his band with him, but they soon departed. In July, Kielbania went off to get married. 'Monk' Blackburn – who had a house in Woodstock – also soon left. The rambling single-storey retreat was an idyll for rustic domesticity and songwriting, providing rehearsal space in a living room with a picture window overlooking a beautiful lake.

Janet Planet told the *Los Angeles Times* in 1998: 'Van would sit in front of a two-track reel-to-reel recorder with a guitar in our living room for hours upon hours upon hours. Then I'd go back and meticulously transcribe his roughed-out lyrics. Slowly but surely, those tapes were honed and refined into beautiful songs'. The atmosphere of the 'arts colony' in Woodstock was also conducive to quiet living, at least for the next few months.

Morrison now needed to hire new musicians to work on the second album he owed to Merenstein's Inherit Productions. Van was also interested in making a record more musically varied than *Astral Weeks* and more likely to attract attention. He didn't yet have specific songs for the album but was writing new ones and revisiting old ones – some of which he'd already demoed and would include on future LPs, such as the R&B album-openers 'Wild Night' and 'Domino'.

The musicians Morrison enlisted included several who later went on to play with him in concert and a number who were to figure in the Caledonia Soul Orchestra. Horn players Jack Schroer and Collin Tilton were recruited from the Colwell-Winfield Blues Band – a group about to break up – who Van knew from Boston. A friend and former bandmate of theirs was also conscripted: bassist John Klingberg. Apple Pie Motherhood Band – another group about to split up – presented pianist and organist Jef Labes. Guitarist John Platania – born near Woodstock – came to Van's attention while playing in a club, and has since gone on to be one of his most trusted collaborators, even co-writing a couple of songs and featuring decades later on Morrison's 2016 album *Keep Me Singing*. After a stint with The Fugs, Bob Mason joined temporarily on drums, and played on some demos and gigs. Drummer/percussionist Gary Mallaber – who was a fan of *Astral Weeks* and was playing with a band called Raven at the time he introduced himself to Morrison in New York at a Café Au Go Go concert in August 1969. The new personnel gave Morrison far more of the R&B feel he wanted, a band he could work up the tracks with, and a backbeat that was absent from the last album.

Though he was living in Woodstock, Morrison was pleased to miss the famous 1969 Music and Art Fair in August, which took place in Bethel: over 50 miles away. But he did appear the following week at one of the Woodstock-Saugerties Sound-Outs: mini-festivals that started in 1967 and were precursors to the more famous and much larger event. He'd also performed at the Newport Folk Festival on 20 July 1969: the day Neil Armstrong became the first person to walk on the moon. A short film exists of Morrison playing a few minutes of a sublime version of 'Madame George', which seems to be the only video of him on stage that year.

In winter and spring 1969, Morrison entered Warner Bros. in New York to rehearse and record. But of the dozen-or-more songs demoed, only 'Come Running' made it to the new album. Other recordings have leaked out on bootlegs, like the love song 'Bit By Bit', the one-minute-long all-night-drinking ditty 'I Can't Get Straight', the pledge 'If I Had A Rainbow', and two odes to girls: 'Lorna', and Sally in 'Hey, Where Are You?'. American singer Roy Head released 'Bit By Bit' as a single in 1972; the Morrison song 'You('ve) Got the Power' appearing on Head's album *Dismal Prisoner* that same year. When a 1970 demo disc went up for auction in 2003, it became clear that these two songs had been pitched to other artists along with the then-unknown 'Coming Down To Joy'. That recording is a fascinating organ-laden track where Morrison speaks the lines in the background. The you-and-me-on-the-backstreets lyric uses some of the phrases Morrison toyed with at this time, such as 'with my poetry and jazz' from the poem on the back of *Astral Weeks*. In 2021, the idea was resuscitated and completely reworked as a piano and sax number for the opening of Kenneth Branagh's film *Belfast*, leading to an Oscar nomination for 'Down to Joy' as Best Original Song.

None of this period's 'lost' demos seem to complement the *Moondance* songs that well, but some phrases are familiar. For example, 'If You Rock Me' has the line about the sun coming up from 'And It Stoned Me', while 'Rock And Roll Band' contains lyrics about softly sighing that were re-used on 'Everyone'. 'Set My Soul On Fire' is another song that was tried out several times, and has familiar phrases about strolling along lanes, while the title line 'Set My Soul On Fire' itself appears at the end of 'I've Been Working' on *His Band and the Street Choir*. More interestingly, some takes – such as the six-minute version of 'Lorna' (aka 'By The River') and the expanded bus-stop story 'Hey, Where Are You?' – echo the sound, mood and sometimes images of *Astral Weeks*. 'Train' – the slow blues demoed at the *Astral Weeks* sessions – was most likely a real contender for inclusion on any follow-up project – a faster outtake called 'On A Rainy Afternoon' (cut in 1969) or 'Train (On A Rainy Afternoon)' starts to sound like a musical fit with *Astral Weeks*, plus its lyric refers to a beautiful child going barefoot by the railroad track. This version certainly suggests the song was among those Morrison said were intended as part of the *Astral Weeks* suite. Another song, 'Magic Night', quotes 'The Way Young Lovers Do' and hinges on a phrase about a magic night that would eventually appear prominently on the *Wavelength* single 'Natalia', but which also reminds the listener of the closing section of 'Moondance'. In the demo lyrics, there are more echoes, allusions and references to familiar Morrison imagery but also to other people's songs. For example, 'Magic Night' contains the words 'I hear the sound of mandolins', quoting from Dimitri Tiomkin's 'Wild Is The Wind' (first recorded by Johnny Mathis in 1957).

More in line with Merenstein's hopes than Morrison's, the overall impression of the sessions from the end of 1968 and the first half of 1969 is of the formative months in the development of another acoustic album with similar instrumentation and imagery to *Astral Weeks*. While that album was recorded in a few sessions, most of its songs had been developed over many months in Boston and something similar was perhaps happening at Warner Bros. up to the summer of 1969, at which point a new direction emerged for the new material that was to make up *Moondance*.

So, with little finished music emerging to Morrison's liking from previous sessions for the new album, musical influences at A&R Studios from September onwards shifted towards countrified R&B and soul, and various styles ranging from gospel to the baroque 'clavinette' used on 'Everyone'. Merenstein began as producer on the Sinatra lounge vibe of 'Moondance' recorded in August, but in the end he was credited on all other tracks as simply 'executive producer'. It seems he lost more and more control as Morrison increasingly took to the helm. Merenstein tried to progress the recording sessions at Century Sound with the musicians who played on *Astral Weeks*, but by now, Morrison had changed personnel, introducing a new rhythm section, horns, and even backing singers on a couple of tracks: including 'Cissy' Houston (mother of Whitney), who'd been one of The Sweet Inspirations singing on 'Brown Eyed Girl'.

The album version of 'Moondance' seems to have been recorded in August at Mastertone Studio on West 42nd Street. The other tracks came together in the following months at A&R on 7th Avenue, and were mixed there, where The Band had recorded some of *Music from Big Pink*. Five engineers worked on *Moondance* – most notably Elliot Scheiner, who started as producer Phil Ramone's assistant at A&R a few years earlier. Scheiner went on to become one of the most respected engineers in the business, working on beautiful sounding albums like Steely Dan's *Aja* (1977), and even inspiring the story behind their 1976 song 'Haitian Divorce' on *The Royal Scam* (an album that has a connection to Morrison, as we'll discuss later).

Scheiner was called back for the *Moondance* remaster in 2013 and explains in the liner notes how the tracks were recorded in mono and mixed to stereo:

Back in those days, we were working mostly with 8-track technology, and the mixing largely took place as you were recording. The drums, for example, were in mono, so you had to balance the toms, kick, hat and snare while you were tracking. Same with backing vocals. I remember that 'Crazy Love' only had six tracks: drums, bass, guitar and vibes had their own tracks, Van had one, and the girls who sang backing vocals had the sixth. You mixed as you recorded, and you had to commit to things as you went along.

The record ended up so different to *Astral Weeks*, yet shone through as another masterpiece – its beauty and variety best appreciated through the sonic clarity of Scheiner's remaster. The opening track, 'And it Stoned Me' is a high-on-nature hymn to the cleansing power of water, and to the free and innocent pleasure of childhood. Its lyric focuses on the memory of a fishing trip Morrison took to Ballystockart as a boy, and his recollection of stopping on the way at a village where he asked a man for a drink of water at an old stone house. The influence of The Band's *Music from Big Pink* is there in the roots feel of this and several other songs – such as 'Caravan', where nature and companionship give life meaning, as opposed to the inner spiritual feelings of *Astral Weeks*. Morrison got to know The Band well while he was in Woodstock – particularly Richard Manuel, and he also got along with Fred Neil, who lived in West Saugerties on the same road as The Band: no doubt influencing Morrison's decision to perform Neil's song 'Everybody's Talkin'' in concert in 1973.

Morrison has said he wrote 'Moondance' on the saxophone as an instrumental in 1965 and it had been around the block a few times before its final version. In 1968 it was considered as a possible *Astral Weeks* track. 'Monk' Blackburn recalls recording the song several times before he quit. As the first track finished in its album version, 'Moondance' is named by Jef Labes as the record's only track that was properly influenced by Merenstein. Perhaps in response to the perfunctory nature of the *Astral Weeks* sessions, new songs like 'Moondance' were tried and recorded dozens of times with different tempos and styles. Labes said it was recognised that the song stood out from the other tracks on the album, partly because the new band nailed it on the first take but largely because its jazz swing made it especially distinctive. The musicians recorded more versions in different styles but on reflection, had it right that first time, not least because of Schroer's iconic alto saxophone solo accompanying Klingberg's walking bass line, Labes' distinctive piano solo, and Tilton's closing flute trill. (Takes 21 and 22 can be heard on the expanded 2013 *Moondance* remaster.) It's the first of the album's love songs, and conveys a staple Morrison scene reiterating the feel of 'The Way Young Lovers Do', but here under Morrison's favourite autumn skies.

'Crazy Love' is a tribute to the comfort and peace of a loving relationship, suggesting the harmony of rural domesticity in 1969. The song is wonderfully sung; high-pitched and up close to the mic, praising a love that makes Van righteous and mellow down in his soul. When drummer Gary Mallaber heard Morrison hit the high falsetto note, he offered to play vibraphone in accompaniment, and the singer encouraged him to experiment – indeed, finding no soft mallets to play the instrument, Mallaber used screwdrivers with rubber handles instead.

In a 2015 *Uncut* article, Mallaber spoke of when Morrison began 'Into The Mystic' on the acoustic guitar and he heard him start to sing:

That's when I knew something extraordinary was happening. We'd messed with it a little bit in Woodstock, but it was nothing like going after it in the studio. It was like the difference between a flight simulator and actually taking off! The hairs on my arms shot up. I was lost in listening to the cut and playing on it at the same time. It was like time-travelling.

'Into The Mystic' has an archetypal Morrison lyric. There are several ambiguities in the opening lines, which could be written in different ways (e.g. born/borne), and the words celebrate a pantheistic union with nature in the face of existential uncertainty. It works equally well as a love song and a song of passing – asserting the mysteries of living and dying, crossing the bar over to somewhere unknown, coming to the end of something and finding it 'too late to stop now'. Suitably, Morrison originally conceived the song as 'Into The Misty'; as sung, the title line can be heard either way.

Oddly, there are two mixes of the track in circulation. The one on the original release is from December 1969 and has Morrison playing tambourine. But when the album was re-pressed, the wrong source master was used, and that later mix from January 1970 was used on pressings for years, without Morrison's tambourine part (This is the more-common version). Among many covers, there are notable versions by Ben E. King, Joe Cocker and The Allman Brothers Band.

The track order for *Moondance* went through several versions, and the original sequence placed both 'And It Stoned Me' and 'Crazy Love' on side two. On the finished LP, however, 'And It Stoned Me' fittingly closes side one after the exuberance of 'Caravan'. The first of Morrison's songs to praise the free spirit of travellers (creating a segue into the gypsy-soul of 'Into The Mystic'), 'Caravan' was partly inspired by Van's new Woodstock setting and the backwoods scenery. He conceived the lyric after hearing a radio playing, despite there being no other house within a mile. It's a paean to music on the airwaves, comradeship, the travelling life, and the primal joy of singing and dancing around a campfire underneath the stars. While the caravan has 'all my friends', the only name-checked characters are Gypsy Robin and Sweet Ammaro: who'd appeared in earlier versions as Amarou, Emma Rose and even Uncle Joe. Originally titled 'Turn It Up', the song became another joyous concert favourite: of which more later.

Side two opens with the lead single and *Billboard* top 40 hit 'Come Running', which continues the album's positive feel, emphasizing joy, love, redemption, and renewed spirit. The lyric takes us back beside the railway tracks to celebrate the sun, wind, rain, dreams and rainbows – in other words, it's a song of innocence and freedom in a classic Morrison setting. There's a hound dog for company, and the lyric foreshadows that of 'Redwood Tree' on *Saint Dominic's Preview*, in which a boy and his dog go out to find a rainbow.

Next comes the classic blues of 'These Dreams Of You': a brassy lullaby led by alto and tenor saxes. Supposedly inspired by Morrison's dream of an assassination attempt on Ray Charles, the lyric is at odds with itself. Upbeat, swaggering music accompanies a series of nightmares of abandonment, betrayal and deceit, contrasting with the soothing bridge saying, 'Don't ever think about it'. The discrepancy between the hush-a-bye reassurance and the chorus asserting that the bad dreams are true, creates an odd and almost comical image of the relationship between the singer, his nightmares of 'you', and the 'angel' being coaxed back to sleep. Morrison has said he doesn't know the meaning of the opening line 'I dreamed you paid your dues in Canada', but it's worth noting that in October 1969, in the midst of recording the album, he played six nights in Ottawa. It's possible the upcoming dates were in his mind when writing the song that summer, though the Canadians who inspired the *next* song could also be responsible for this dream about working north of the border. There is another intriguing connection: Morrison visited an aunt in Toronto in 1959, and she sneaked the teenage Van into a club to see Canadian rock singer Ronnie Hawkins. Morrison told his biographer Ritchie Yorke that what Hawkins and his band The Hawks were doing on stage that night was exactly what *he* wanted to be doing. While this was a year before Robbie Robertson joined The Hawks – let alone any of the other Canadian members of what would become The Band – the American paying his dues on the drums would've been Levon Helm.

The uplifting gospel of 'Brand New Day' was prompted by hearing The Band on the radio, almost certainly playing their version of Dylan's 'I Shall Be Released', which Morrison would sing at the mic with Dylan and Robbie Robertson at The Band's *The Last Waltz* concert on Thanksgiving Day 1976. Morrison has said 'Brand New Day' is the album's track that was most clearly developed as a successful execution of his original idea. The lyric strongly echoes the sentiment of Dylan's song – a wave of joy in freedom from adversity and a new dawn of emancipation. Unlike The Band's roots version of Dylan's song on *Music from Big Pink*, 'Brand New Day' aspires to the status of a Southern spiritual, with the backing singers operating as a small choir. 'I Shall Be Released' suggests the resentment of wrongful imprisonment; its key image of 'seeing a light come shining' being one Morrison was also drawn to. Dylan's song is ambiguous and may refer to a release from jail or from life, but Morrison's is primarily about personal regeneration and spiritual illumination – a theme evident across his 1970s songs, if most well-known from 1989's 'Whenever God Shines His Light'.

Following the run of largely piano-based songs, 'Everyone' is driven by acoustic guitar, and has a startling 'clavinette' opening. It's the album's fastest song and culminates in a rare flute solo from Collin Tilton. Said to be a song of hope, it features walks and dreams, like several *Astral Weeks* songs, all along the lane and the avenue and the stream.

'Glad Tidings' ends the album in a tribute to the powerful surprise that can happen when you meet people halfway. With the first three lines unusually opening with the word 'And', 'Glad Tidings' *appears* to be a song of blessings, perhaps like when the word on your loved one's lips is 'Christmas'. The lyric's origin lay in a couple of letters sent between London and New York with 'Glad tidings' written on the envelope. Though composed of sentences that seem to be a string of non-sequiturs, the lyric recognises and accepts the unexpected – don't read between the lines, 'open up your eyes', 'come in right on time'. It can be seen as a standard Morrison lyric about connecting with love, peace, and persuasion. But it can also be read as a bitter song about being taken advantage of – a warning about the music business, where you can proceed with good intentions and then discover yourself rudely fleeced, which is what Morrison found as an artist on both sides of the Atlantic. With identical opening and closing lines, it's a great slice of uptempo R&B carried along by the brass section to close the album triumphantly and underline the diversity of the ten songs.

Where *Astral Weeks* has a singular feel, the breadth of style on *Moondance* is, in contrast, wide indeed. Each track seems to almost be in a different genre, and yet the record doesn't feel like a mixed bag. The title song strikes some listeners as having a different sound, but the variety of approaches means no track is like any other. Some of the recordings have achieved classic status, and several became FM rotation plays immediately, especially on the West Coast. For many listeners, there is not a weak link on the record.

Another fine composition, the slow-build little-boy-lost song 'Really Don't Know' would have to wait for release on the 1998 outtake compilation *The Philosopher's Stone*. Its piano-based white soul suggests how Morrison influenced the Jersey Shore Sound, and the recording could sit neatly alongside Southside Johnny and the Asbury Jukes' version of Bruce Springsteen's 'The Fever' and the Jukes' cover of Solomon Burke's 'Got To Get You Off Of My Mind' on their 1976 debut album. After the horns kick in about a quarter of the way through 'Really Don't Know', Morrison beautifully uses space and silence to heighten the tension to a crescendo alongside his vocal gymnastics.

Around the time of *Moondance*, an early demo was made of 'Wonderful Remark', a song included on *The Philosopher's Stone* in its full eight-minute glory, utilising a melody reworked from the song 'Joe Harper Saturday Morning' recorded during the Bang sessions. A shorter version featuring Robbie Robertson and Nicky Hopkins first aired in Scorsese's 1982 film *The King of Comedy*, and appeared on *The Best of Van Morrison* in 1990. Both songs are among Morrison's best, but they are somewhat downbeat in tone, unlike the mainly upbeat R&B songs he put out at the time: perhaps indicating why they didn't suit either of the two 1970 albums.

Morrison headed back to Woodstock for Christmas at the end of recording *Moondance*, leaving Scheiner and Mallaber to mix the album. Liner notes in the form of 'A Fable' were supplied by Janet Planet, who appeared as a backing vocalist on the next three albums. Meanwhile, the cover shots were taken by iconic Woodstock chronicler Elliott Landy, who'd also snapped photographs for Bob Dylan's *Nashville Skyline* and The Band's *Music from Big Pink*.

Moondance was well received by Warner Bros., who renewed Morrison's contract. The album was also well-received critically and commercially, drawing praise from Bangs and Marcus again. Unlike the brilliant but out-of-step *Astral Weeks*, it blended well with the music of the times, from the acoustic singer-songwriter upsurge to the groundswell of Americana fronted by The Band ('Country soul' journalist Al Aronowitz called it at the time). Several tracks became FM radio staples in the States, and the songs were covered by a number of artists, including Esther Phillips, Rita Coolidge and Helen Reddy, who all recorded versions of 'Crazy Love'.

Over the decades, *Moondance* has featured in many greatest hits album lists, usually only topped by *Astral Weeks* in Morrison's canon, while representing the breadth of his music far more than that earlier singular album. In addition to the revelatory remix, the 2013 2-CD expanded release supplies bonuses in the form of two Morrison originals – the previously unreleased 'I Shall Sing', and an early version of the *His Band and the Street Choir* song 'I've Been Working' (of which the 4-CD deluxe issue even includes two versions over ten minutes long). It also includes a recording of the blues standard 'Nobody Knows You When You're Down and Out', another version of which appeared on Derek and the Dominos' classic 1970 album *Layla and Other Assorted Love Songs*. Though Morrison found it surplus to his own requirements in 1970, the infectious 'I Shall Sing' appeared that year on the album *Keep Me in Mind* by Miriam Makeba (which also has a version of 'Brand New Day'). A song recorded quite a few times, it was also included on Art Garfunkel's 1973 album *Angel Clare*, and on *Toots and the Maytals* 1976 album, *Reggae Got Soul*.

Morrison did little to promote *Moondance* in the media, as he'd been burned too often by journalists, but he toured with Labes, Tilton, Platania, Klingberg, and Schroer. Mallaber started out with the touring band but left after a few gigs because Raven had secured a record deal. Consequently, Mason returned briefly, but then the band was joined by new drummer David Shaw (Dahaud Shaar) – who Morrison had seen playing in Woodstock. At the gigs, Morrison delivered a tight set of *Moondance* tracks, plus 'Brown Eyed Girl' and some songs from *Astral Weeks*, building to the extended driving, brassy showpiece of 'Cyprus Avenue', which sometimes topped 12 minutes. However, the band didn't visit many cities, and Morrison preferred smaller venues. There was also little organised effort to take the material to new places, so the concerts were mostly on the East or West Coasts. Canada was the only country Morrison played outside the US until mid-1973.

Scant live 1970 movie footage exists, but there is a great two-song official segment with a truncated version of 'These Dreams of You' and an extended 'Cyprus Avenue' at the Fillmore East, introduced by Bill Graham. The New York show on 23 September 1970 also included The Byrds, The Elvin Bishop Group, and The Allman Brothers, among others, and was originally filmed by National Educational Television as the TV special *Welcome To Fillmore East.* Morrison also appears in Bert Tenzer's *The Day the Music Died* – a documentary about the 1970 New York 'Festival': three concerts at Downing Stadium, Randall's Island, that ran from 17-19 July. Morrison is shown performing 'Come Running' and there's a snippet of 'Cyprus Avenue'. The film is predominantly the story of the rise of activism and the end of the hippy dream at the close of the 1960s. Before the festival began, local militant groups from the black and Puerto Rican communities held the organisers to ransom. Thousands gatecrashed the concerts, and some bands decided not to turn up. By the time Morrison played on the Sunday, it was unclear if anyone would get paid. The concerts were a financial disaster, and Morrison's set was interrupted twice – first by the crowd, and then by Van himself in an attempt to get the audience's attention. Promoter Don Friedman said, 'The festival spirit is dead, and it happened quickly. I don't know the reasons why – greed on everyone's part, I guess. The love/peace thing of Woodstock is out. Anarchy. Complete and total anarchy. That's what's replaced it'. The same month, Morrison appeared on the cover of *Rolling Stone* for the first time: a black-and-white shot of him singing in shades.

Following the album's success, new manager Mary Martin was getting Morrison's financial and publishing affairs sorted, with Van cutting ties with Merenstein-Schwaid's Inherit Productions but staying with Warner Bros.. The success of *Moondance* put him in a viable position to develop his career without the previously onerous contractual burdens and severe financial constraints.

His Band and the Street Choir (1970)

Personnel:
Van Morrison: vocals, guitar, harmonica; tenor saxophone ('Crazy Face', 'Call Me Up In Dreamland')
Alan Hand: piano, Hammond organ, celeste
Keith Johnson: trumpet, Hammond Organ
John Klingberg: bass
John Platania: lead and rhythm guitar, mandolin

Jack Schroer: piano, saxophone

Dahaud Shaar (David Shaw): drums, bass clarinet, percussion, backing vocals

Janet Planet, Martha Velez, Larry Goldsmith, Andrew Robinson, Ellen Schroer: backing vocals

Jackie Verdell, Emily 'Cissy' Houston, Judy Clay: backing vocals ('If I Ever Needed Someone')

Producer: Van Morrison

All songs by Van Morrison

Recorded at A&R Studios New York, March-July 1970

Release date: US: November 1970, UK: January 1971

Chart places: US: 32, UK: 18

Running time: 42:22

Tracklisting: Side One: 1. 'Domino', 2. 'Crazy Face', 3. 'Give Me A Kiss', 4. 'I've Been Working', 5. 'Call Me Up In Dreamland', 6. 'I'll Be Your Lover, Too'. Side Two: 1. 'Blue Money', 2. 'Virgo Clowns', 3. 'Gypsy Queen', 4. 'Sweet Jannie', 5. 'If I Ever Needed Someone', 6. 'Street Choir'

Morrison's band continued to experiment with new material and fresh takes on old as-yet-unreleased songs. Some demos were recorded with basic equipment in a small church Shaar found in Woodstock. According to Labes, songs came fairly easily to Morrison, who would record a tune on guitar into a tape recorder, and play it back to come up with lyrics. However, April shows in San Francisco at the Fillmore West and Winterland confirmed the fact that small bursts of road gigs were not suiting Morrison nor Labes well. While he would return for a run of mid-1970s albums, Labes decided to quit the group. Meanwhile, alongside other factors, West Coast appreciation for Morrison's music probably encouraged him to think it might be a better place to live.

Originally titled *Virgo's Fool* in homage to its singer's sun sign, *His Band and the Street Choir* was imagined as a largely *a cappella* record at a time when street-corner singing had become popular in the working-class quarters of US cities – though Morrison would've had the tradition of Belfast street singing firmly in mind. In the end, the album came across as a continuation of the approach on *Moondance,* but with greater use of instrumentation and vocal harmonies. Morrison says the idea of the Street Choir didn't turn out as he had envisaged, with extra members joining the quartet he'd specifically wanted. Engineer Elliot Scheiner was again at the controls but was soon eased to the sidelines, with Morrison producing the record, assisted by percussionist Shaar. *His Band and the Street Choir* is a blend of archetypal Morrison subjects and fresh love songs to Van's wife and daughter (Shana – whom the singer would go on to duet in later years – was born between the two 1970 releases). Janet Planet provided not only backing vocals, but sleeve notes again and she also designed the cover. The six members of the street choir feature heavily (Shaar, Planet, Velez, Goldsmith, Robinson and Schroer), though the smoothest backing vocals come from the returning trio of Houston, Verdell, and Clay on 'If I Ever Needed Someone'.

Recorded in two bursts in the spring and summer of 1970, *His Band and the Street Choir* leads off with the R&B single 'Domino'. By now, an old song, 'Domino' had been through several styles and lyrics before reaching its definitive version as an uptempo tribute to Fats Domino: the man Elvis Presley dubbed 'The real king of rock 'n' roll' – though Fats himself once said, 'What they call rock 'n' roll now is rhythm and blues'. Among the numerous bootleg versions of 'Domino', there's an acoustic, largely *a cappella* take, that perhaps indicates the album's original street-choir harmony concept, with just voices, handclaps, and guitar. The lyric – featuring a man with a dog, a girl with long blonde hair – is predominantly *not* about Fats Domino but about singing the song itself. It began as an odd acoustic tryout with a lyric about a man in whose house the singer and his friends would go to have fun; it ended up as a radio-friendly Domino tribute after incorporating lines from the lost Morrison composition 'Down In The Maverick' (which was apparently about the Maverick colony Hervey White started for radical artists in Woodstock). From this unpromising history came a US hit single.

While Schroer played saxophone on the album, 'Crazy Face' (and 'Call Me Up In Dreamland') features Morrison on tenor sax. One of several of his songs referring to Jesse James (including the 'Going Around With Jesse James' *Astral Weeks* outtake), 'Crazy Face' repeats two four-line verses suggesting a showdown, with the character arriving at church, dressed in classic western garb – black satin suit and lace – carrying the outlaw's .38-calibre handgun. Along with Morrison's lifelong interest in the West, it may be one of the songs that led The Band to nickname him The Belfast Cowboy – an echo of Lead Belly's 'Western Cowboy' – and Morrison does go on to appear in black suit, white shirt, and big black bow tie on the sleeve of his next album. Jesse James was known to mostly carry a .44-calibre and then a Colt .45, so the reference to a .38 may be generic. James was also reputed to carry upwards of a dozen pistols, and by the time he died in 1882, a .38 like the Colt 1851 Navy Revolver could've been among them. The song ends abruptly, as if the shoot-out has just suddenly occurred. The lyric could be linked to the cowboy-song tradition most successfully commercialised by Marty Robbins on his 1959 album *Gunfighter Ballads and Trail Songs*, though Morrison's touchstones were more likely Jimmie Rodgers' 'Blue Yodel No. 1' and Lead Belly's 'When I Was A Cowboy'. After this, it's not a long stretch from Rodgers' 'I'm gonna shoot poor Thelma/Just to see her jump and fall' or indeed Johnny Cash's more famous 'I shot a man in Reno just to watch him die', to Linden Arden taking the law into his own hands and living with a gun in San Francisco on *Veedon Fleece*.

'Give Me A Kiss' is doo-wop party music, followed by the *Moondance* and *Astral Weeks* try-out 'I've Been Working': a blue-collar song with the same sentiment as The Beatles' 'A Hard Day's Night', but with James Brown funk. Morrison delivers the lyric from the pulpit to someone who'll not just make him feel alright but set his soul on fire (as also in the later B-side 'You've Got The Power'). A tight rhythm section drives the track until a minute in when the horns ignite it and the full band explodes, complementing the stunning vocal. The alternative version on the 2015 remaster features an extra section of scorching brass work that was sadly absent from the final cut but reveals how the song would go on to work so well in concert.

Strongly featuring the Street Choir, 'Call Me Up In Dreamland' is a southern gospel tribute to the radio and to life on the road, and would've showcased the originally-planned *a cappella* approach. It was released as a single in 1971, with 'Street Choir' as the B-side, but it didn't light up the charts. 'I'll Be Your Lover, Too' – the ballad closing side one – matches *Moondance's* 'Crazy Love' for beauty and emotion. Consisting of just bass, guitar and drums, it would not have been out of place on *Astral Weeks*.

Like 'Domino' on side one, 'Blue Money' opens side two in a catchy radio-friendly style. A less-successful single (b/w 'Sweet Thing'), it still reached the US top 30. Another slice of R&B aimed at the clubs, it's a funky get-up-and-get-down dance track, led by the horn section punctuating the vocal – Morrison singing about his 'honey' earning cash by posing for seedy photos: juice money.

Intended to complement the original album title *Virgo's Fool*, 'Virgo Clowns' was another old song, originally titled '(Sit Down) Funny Face'. Known to be performed as early as shows at Boston's Catacombs nightclub billed as the 'Van Morrison Controversy' in 1968, it's a song about the healing power of love and play: 'Let your laughter fill the room'.

With lovely mandolin playing from Platania, it's perhaps an unlikely lullaby, and in that regard, is similar to 'These Dreams Of You'.

The largely falsetto 'Gypsy Queen' opens with Hand on celeste, joined by bass and acoustic guitar before the full band pitches in. When the other musicians fade out after three minutes, the celeste returns, sounding like a musical box. The lyric makes it this album's 'Caravan' track about dancing beneath the stars, with familiar images of love in the rain beneath the summer moon. It also introduces the line 'Let your love come tumblin' down': so close to the repeated phrase that opens 'Listen To The Lion'.

'Sweet Jannie' is another 12-bar blues – pleasant but unremarkable, like 'Give Me A Kiss'. 'If I Ever Needed Someone' reveals Morrison's love of gospel and sweet soul. It reprises the 'Brand New Day' sentiment of a guiding light leading through darkness to a 'new tomorrow', from 'the long, lonely night', into the dawn. It was first attempted at Warner Bros. in spring 1969, in the gap between *Astral Weeks* and *Moondance*.

The great closing track 'Street Choir' suggests a different path the project might've taken. A song about refusing to accept back someone who betrayed the singer by leaving America when times were hard, it features Keith Johnson's superb trumpet work and the excellent harmonica playing for which Morrison is rarely given sufficient credit. Led by church organ and vocals, 'Street Choir' is the album's longest track, though it's still under five minutes long and yearns for the expansive treatment that came on Morrison's late-1970s albums. It points beyond *Tupelo Honey* to *Saint Dominic's Preview*, where the music from 'Street Choir' would've sat wonderfully.

Van seems to be working here – as on *Moondance* – on shorter songs with single potential. John Platania has said that Morrison was looking for hooks at the time, while one of the best recordings from the sessions was a jam known as 'Caledonia Soul Music', which was not put on the album, but was passed to Bay Area radio station KSAN to play at will. (There are two versions: one around 16 minutes long, and a more-polished take at just over 17 minutes). A track encompassing Morrison's long-form feel from the 1970s through to early-1980s albums like *Beautiful Vision*, it is a meditative instrumental that must've contributed to the inspiration behind the Caledonia Soul Orchestra. It's Morrison's first use of the word 'Caledonia' in a title, though his association with the name will have gone back to his childhood *and* – musically – to Louis Jordan's 'Caldonia': released the year Morrison was born (1945) and released by Van as a single in 1974.

His Band and the Street Choir was well-received and even topped *Moondance* by having a top ten US single in 'Domino': Morrison's highest-placed hit. But the tracks don't quite cohere into a classic album the way those on *Moondance* do, and several songs are leftovers from earlier sessions or are underdeveloped new tracks. There is some excellent R&B here, and essential Morrison recordings such as 'I'll Be Your Lover, Too' and 'Virgo Clowns', with only a couple of songs that perhaps could've been shelved. Arguably, the record lacks the organic identity of the two previous records, even though in the album photographs, Warner Bros. promoted the sense of a down-on-the-ranch or backwoods project in the mould of The Band.

The album turned out to be Morrison's highest-charting 1970s record in the UK as well as a great success in the US. It also came at a relatively contented time for him after the difficulties of the late-1960s. Hindsight places it as a very good record, though it was somewhat rushed, as Warner Bros. wanted singles material to get the LP out before Christmas and to capitalise on the *Moondance* success. The 2015 remaster is again impressive (if not quite the revelation the earlier 1970 album's remaster proved to be), and supplies alternative takes or versions of five of the album's tracks.

At the time the album was released in November 1970, Morrison was displeased with the way his music was being packaged. Extra backing singers had been added to the four Street Choir members he'd envisaged, the album title was changed after he delivered the tapes (in the US, the cover originally showed no title), the running order was altered, side one ended with studio talk, the track list was initially wrong on promo copies, and the cover photo made him look like a hippy. Janet Planet designed the cover and wrote sleeve notes, so some of the discrepancies will have been down to their different emphases for his image. The gatefold band shots by respected photographer David Gahr (see his 1968 book with Robert Shelton: *The Face of Folk Music*) reflected the feel of the album title, though the photographs were actually taken at a birthday party for Planet's son.

As the year ended, change was in the air once more. The east would soon be left behind as the idea of relocating out west loomed larger. There were good reasons for a move, given how Woodstock had changed after the festival. Planet's life had been based in California before she met Van, and the last year had made it more apparent that the West Coast was where Morrison's biggest fan base resided.

1971: Tupelo Honey

Tupelo Honey (1971)

Personnel:

Van Morrison: rhythm guitar, harmonica, vocals

Ronnie Montrose: guitars, mandolin, backing vocals

Luis Gasca: trumpet

Connie Kay: drums ('Starting A New Life', 'Tupelo Honey', 'When That Evening Sun Goes Down', 'Old Old Woodstock')

Rick Shlosser: drums

Bill Church: bass

Bruce Royston: flute

'Boots' Houston: flute, backing vocal

Mark Jordan: piano

Gary Mallaber: percussion, vibraphone

John McFee: pedal steel guitar

Ted Templeman: organ ('Tupelo Honey')

Janet Planet, Ellen Schroer: backing vocals

Jack Schroer: saxophones

Producers: Van Morrison, Ted Templeman

All songs by Van Morrison

Recorded at Wally Heider Studios and Columbia Studios in San Francisco, spring-summer 1971

Release date: US: October 1971, UK: November 1971

Chart places: US: 27, UK -

Running time: 40:42

Tracklisting: Side One: 1. 'Wild Night', 2. '(Straight To Your Heart) Like A Cannonball', 3. 'Old Old Woodstock', 4. 'Starting A New Life', 5. 'You're My Woman'. Side Two: 1. 'Tupelo Honey', 2. 'I Wanna Roo You (Scottish Derivative)', 3. 'When That Evening Sun Goes Down', 9. 'Moonshine Whiskey'

The first Morrison recorded performance of 1971 appeared on someone else's album. When he dropped in on The Band at Albert Grossman's recently-opened Bearsville Studios near Woodstock, they taped a song called '4% Pantomime', which appeared on the group's fourth album *Cahoots*. Morrison and drinking buddy Richard Manuel trade vocals in this stirring roots song about two whisky-slugging, poker-playing musicians in L.A.: presumably the singers themselves during the recording of *The Band* (1969). The song title supposedly refers to the alcohol

difference between Johnnie Walker Red and Black labels, whisky-drinking
leading to the drunken pantomime sketched out in puns and rhymes.
This is also where the nickname Belfast Cowboy is heard for the first
time, amid the slightly slurred singing and playing. While Manuel sings
the song fairly straight, Van, in comparison, plays on the drunken scene,
his phrasing often intentionally at odds with the song. Morrison shared
writing credit with The Band's Robbie Robertson.

Van also played some gigs late that winter, ending with a couple of
shows at the soon-to-close Fillmore in New York as a farewell to the East
Coast and a warm-up to a possible European tour. The Fillmore concerts
suggested he was unwilling to play the rock star for those of his new
audience attracted by his recent singles' success. European dates would've
taken him to Belfast and London's Royal Festival Hall. Reportedly he was
also lined up for a BBC *In Concert* show: delivered around that time by
the likes of Carole King, Neil Young, James Taylor, and Joni Mitchell. In
May, the British press announced the tour was off, by which time Morrison
had also left Woodstock.

By the end of winter 1971, it was clear Morrison was moving 3000
miles away, and the band that played on *Street Choir* would need to
consider their future. The previous year's concert film of the Festival
meant Woodstock was no longer just an artistic haven but had become
a frequent stop-off on the hippy trail. Morrison also said he liked the
positive atmosphere of the West Coast music scene.

Whatever the main motivation for the move, a house in Fairfax – north
of San Francisco – was to become home. With a population of about
75,000, the town was very near San Anselmo, and only three miles from
San Rafael, which would both feature in the opening track of *Hard Nose
the Highway* in 1973. The new house was a rural retreat among redwood
trees and oaks, on an acre of land in the hills of Marin County.

Recording of a new album was expected, for which a new band was
needed. Some familiar players were enlisted, but a number of new
West Coast musicians were hired. Warner Bros. house producer Ted
Templeman was assigned to oversee the San Francisco sessions. The
first were at the Wally Heider Studios, where significant albums such as
Grateful Dead's *American Beauty* and Neil Young's *Everybody Knows This
Is Nowhere* were recorded. The musicians rehearsed on their own before
Morrison was picked up from his hotel to lead the definitive cuts.

Most significantly, Morrison was joined on guitar and mandolin by
future rocker Ronnie Montrose, who brought with him Sawbuck bassist

Bill Church. Other fresh additions were pianist Mark Jordan of the Edison Electric Band, and John McFee on pedal steel from local band Clover (who would back Elvis Costello on his debut album *My Aim is True* (1977)). Jack Schroer continued on saxophone, alongside new flautists Bruce Royston and 'Boots' Houston, and jazz trumpeter Luis Gasca. Janet Planet and Ellen Schroer sang backing vocals, as did many of the players. For the later sessions, Connie Kay (from *Astral Weeks*) sat in on drums, and Gary Mallaber (from *Moondance)* returned on vibes and percussion. Before Kay joined, the album versions of 'Wild Night', 'I Wanna Roo You', 'Moonshine Whiskey', and '(Straight To Your Heart) Like A Cannonball' were recorded with session drummer Rick Shlosser, who was not booked for the subsequent sessions, though he came in for the late addition 'You're My Woman', and would return for *Saint Dominic's Preview* (1972).

The new album turned out to be another selection of original Van compositions to be titled *Tupelo Honey*. However, Morrison might just as easily have made a covers album as he had reportedly cut demos in Woodstock, including Hank Thompson's 'The Wild Side Of Life', Buck Owens' 'Crying Time' and the traditional 'Banks Of The Ohio'. Morrison has since said his intention was to make a country and western album and that the consistent feel of *Tupelo Honey* became diluted by too many leftover songs: presumably meaning tracks like 'Wild Night' and 'When The Evening Sun Goes Down'.

The genre separation – so important to some – was not so significant to Morrison, partly because he took in all kinds of music growing up, *and* 'the beat thing' from Kerouac to Ginsberg. What struck Van most about blues and jazz was timing, and this appreciation of how to use spacing and phrasing applies to all his recordings. In 2015, he told *Uncut*: 'It's all about breaking it up. I don't know about loud guitar music, but for singers, it's about playing with time. Same for jazz. How do you carve up the time, stretch it out; how do you bridge it, how do you make space. It's all about creating space'. Certain songs on *Tupelo Honey* illustrate the point – the more interesting numbers ('You're My Woman', 'Moonshine Whiskey' 'Tupelo Honey') all requiring space and time to unfold stellar vocal performances on recordings lasting over six minutes.

Two sets of sessions in San Francisco yielded *Tupelo Honey* – the first at Wally Heider, mentioned above, and the second at Columbia Studios, where 'When The Evening Sun Goes Down', 'Old Old Woodstock', 'Tupelo Honey', 'Starting A New Life' and 'You're My Woman' were recorded along with the definitive take of 'Listen To The Lion' that would appear on *Saint Dominic's Preview*. Also recorded at Columbia around this time – with Church, Montrose, Connie Kay, and pianist Mark Naftalin – was 'Ordinary People': a song about self-reliance and peace of mind. The recording wasn't officially released until its inclusion on the 1998 compilation of unreleased tracks *The Philosopher's Stone*. Morrison recorded it again – with Jeff Beck and Chris Farlowe in the band – for his 2017 album *Roll With The Punches*.

Most of the *Tupelo Honey* songs were written in Woodstock. 'Wild Night' was an older reworked composition once said to be written in New York. Curiously, playing the song in concert in the 1970s, Morrison interspersed lines from 'Slim Slow Slider', possibly linking the two narratives about stepping out on the streets, though one is an excited celebration of evenings out, and the other a sombre early-morning song. Van conceived 'Wild Night' as a slower number and continued to think of it that way. It was Ronnie Montrose who introduced the distinctive opening guitar hook. While Morrison's original made it into the top 30, a version by John Mellencamp and Meshell Ndegeocello reached the Billboard top three in 1994. In the 1970s, notable cover versions were released by Martha Reeves and Richie Havens. Curiously, Reeves' version – a few years after Morrison's – eschews the original's guitar phrasing and emerges as a vocal-led celebration resting on piano, horns and handclaps. Tim Young's welcome 2008 *Tupelo Honey* remaster also includes an alternative take of 'Wild Night'.

'(Straight To Your Heart) Like A Cannonball' is the first song to suggest the record's concerns with nature, home and hearth. It's also a love song, and domestic harmony is the album's main theme. Montrose's guitar fills, the soft flutes and catchy vocal refrain helped the song's selection as the album's third single. Acoustic guitars and flutes lead a country and western waltz, and the simple lyric could be as much about Fairfax as Woodstock. The single's B-side was 'Old Old Woodstock': another tribute to home life. The lyric is about coming home, like 'I've Been Working', but with the emphasis on peaceful domesticity rather than making love. It paints a simple picture of driving back from a gig or the studio in New York two hours away; feeling the cool night breeze, seeing home in the shady trees, and returning to the family.

'Starting A New Life' harks back to the theme of a fresh beginning evoked most potently on the last album's 'Brand New Day'. Morrison's excellent harmonica-playing is to the forefront, and the lyric is distinctly of the moment because it seems to set out a manifesto for the new beginning in San Francisco. The song is also significant for its use of the phrase 'way on down the line', which was to morph into the key refrain that shimmers up and down at the conclusion of 'Almost Independence Day': the synaesthetic song about premonitions and echoes in the San Francisco Bay that closes *Saint Dominic's Preview*. 'You're My Woman' is also linked to that album, being a late addition that replaced the centrepiece of *Saint Dominic's Preview* 'Listen To The Lion'. Written at the piano during the recording of *Tupelo Honey*, 'You're My Woman' is a blues-ballad hymn to a loving relationship. It's also one of several songs on the album that rely on repetition and accentuation by concentrating on keywords from which Morrison extracts every nuance through soulful vocal intonation. The lyric uses stock visual images to suggest the realisation of love, invoking eyes, lights, and sunshine, plus the new phrase 'really real': an old philosophical expression, then recently familiar from pop songs like 'It's Really Real' (1966) by husband-and-wife duo Jim and Jean.

Squeezing meaning from repeated words and familiar phrases is doubly true of the title track and masterpiece 'Tupelo Honey' – a tribute to American freedom, the sweetness of love, Elvis' birthplace, and the mild honey of the Mississippi-area trees. A ballad showcasing Morrison's vocal abilities, it's been covered by the likes of Cassandra Wilson and Dusty Springfield (using the extra third verse Morrison forgot to sing himself). As a classic Morrison track, it immediately feels (like 'Moondance') as if it's a standard rather than an original. The familiarity is because the melody for the song was borrowed from another much-covered Morrison original, 'Crazy Love', but the emotional effect here comes from the power and conviction of the simultaneously exultant and aching emotions of the singing. The song is a tribute to a beloved woman – whether wife or daughter – but it's also about American liberty. The first verse may allude to the Boston Tea Party. The second explicitly talks about unstoppable forces on the road to freedom – noting men in granite (possibly Mount Rushmore), and others determined to do right through a sense of conviction or honour. The missing verse refers to waiting on 'my number' to go to 'old Manhattan', and suggests the expectation of the immigrant wanting to travel from Europe to the land of the free, sailing past the Statue of Liberty. If the album has an overall thematic link, it's the sweetness of love but also of freedom. *Tupelo Honey* celebrates the country and western music traditions of the southern states – traced back to Europe – and 'Tupelo Honey' arguably celebrates the sweetness of freedom through American independence: a reading of the song heightened by the presence of 'Almost Independence Day' on Morrison's next album.

Flute, steel guitar and mandolin underpin the next domestic love song: the waltz 'I Wanna Roo You (Scottish Derivative)'. A blend of Caledonia and country and western, it's been covered by several female artists, including Goldie Hawn, Jackie De Shannon, and British singer Rumer. The opening line about the 23rd of December being covered in snow, echoes a line from James Taylor's 'Sweet Baby James' released the previous year: 'Now the first of December was covered with snow'. 'Roo' may be a simple play on 'woo', but the common meaning – local to Orkney and Shetland – is to strip a sheep's wool by hand. It could also be considered an alternative to the archaic Scottish word for love: 'loo' or 'lou' (Familiar in songs like 'Skip To My Lou': recorded by – among many others – Lead Belly).

The older 'When That Evening Sun Goes Down' was first demoed at Warner Bros. in New York in 1968 and then attempted again in 1969. Here it barrels along with a honky-tonk piano and almost has the feel of a rag, perhaps worked up through time spent with The Band. A distant good-time cousin to '4% Pantomime', this take even ends with the band chuckling. An alternative version appeared as the B-side to 'Wild Night'. On *Tupelo Honey* it segues smoothly into 'Moonshine Whiskey': a song Morrison says he wrote for someone 'like Janis Joplin' – presumably the kind of character who represents hard-livin', good-lovin' southern comfort. It might also be that he thought the intense and powerful delivery – with its playful bubbles, water, and fish sound effects – would suit Texan Joplin's impassioned and soulful vocal style. The song could even be taken as a simple tribute to the Woodstock queen Joplin, who died in October 1970, but we can also note that Janet Planet was born in Corpus Christi, Texas. The song references the Muscle Shoals classic 'Funky Broadway': most well-known from Wilson Pickett's 1967 top ten-hit version. One of the album's longest tracks, 'Moonshine Whiskey', features the band speeding up to an uncharacteristically abrupt conclusion and its frenetic ending made it a concert favourite.

Even more than its predecessor, *Tupelo Honey* has simple lyrics, and while there are still some fine turns of phrase, the chief pleasure lies in how the words scan with the melodies. The songs have a consistent feel, and the production suits the music, giving a satisfying unity. It was an early production job for Ted Templeman, who gained production credit on the next Morrison album and the live *It's Too Late to Stop Now*, before moving on to work with other artists, including Van Halen and Nicolette Larsen. He also produced the first two Montrose albums in 1973 and 1974. Though Templeman had worked on The Doobie Brothers' debut a little earlier (at which time Warner Bros. GM Joe Smith introduced him to Morrison in Fairfax), he felt *Tupelo Honey* effectively gave him his production break. He remembers the sessions warmly, remarking that he went through three engineers because it was so hard to keep up with Morrison. Templeman says that what he primarily learned from Van was the importance of the artist's process, coming to realise that Morrison liked to record in one take, with minimal overdubs (usually horns and backing vocals). Templeman also appreciated Ronnie Montrose's upbeat influence, which led to his enthusiasm to work with him when the guitarist set up his own band.

The cover photographs by Michael Maggid convey the album's broad C&W/soul appeal, but they were certainly a construct rather than a reflection of Van's reality. The photos were shot in the woods near a friend's farm, where the inner-sleeve picture was set up beside the corral. Ed Thrasher (who worked on *Astral Weeks*) was the art director, and the images express a down-country domesticity that works well with the mood of the album, in the same way, Joel Brodsky's stylised and impressionistic photographs did for the *Astral Weeks* cover. If the *Tupelo Honey* cover had a precursor, it would be Bob Dylan's 1970 album *New Morning*, the cover of which has a similar design and palette with a single portrait and a thick muted border, like a framed picture.

Morrison commented that the *Tupelo Honey* cover was like a painting – not to be confused with the artist's actual life. He also thought the album wasn't fresh and it was filled out with too many old songs. But the record stacks up well against other countrified releases of the time (like Neil Young's *Harvest*, *Eagles*, and James Taylor's *Sweet Baby James*), having a more raw sound, a greater style range, and a lean towards the rootsy late-1960s work of The Band and Dylan – though Morrison's influences will have been better represented by his stage work at the time. If there was a good precedent for the country covers idea, it lay with Ray Charles' 1962 album *Modern Sounds in Country and Western Music* – the influential forerunner in terms of a singer melding blues, jazz, soul, country, gospel. Charles and Morrison were later to duet on a new recording of 'Crazy Love' on Charles' posthumously-released 2004 album *Genius Loves Company*.

The country and western covers album idea surfaced in Morrison's early-1970s concerts. But 'Down By The Riverside' is the only one that's been released in a studio version: as a bonus on the remastered *Tupelo Honey*. At the time, Morrison experimented with a big brassy version of Hank Williams' 'Hey, Good Lookin'' (on Volume II of *It's Too Late to Stop Now*), 'Jambalaya' (later recorded with Linda Gail Lewis for the 2000 album *You Win Again*), 'The Wild Side Of Life', the Patti Page hit 'Tennessee Waltz', Webb Pierce's 'More And More', and songs that cross genres, such as Lead Belly's 'Goodnight Irene', Woody Guthrie's 'Dead Or Alive', The Everly Brothers' 'Let It Be Me', and even '(There'll Be Bluebirds Over) The White Cliffs Of Dover'. Several of these were demoed but remain unreleased. Some songs have appeared on later albums – like 'Dead Or Alive' and 'Goodnight Irene' on *The Skiffle Sessions*, and 'More And More' on *Pay the Devil*. A traditional spiritual, 'Down By The Riverside' (equally known as 'Ain't Gonna Study War No More') dates back to the American Civil War and was often used as a Vietnam anti-war anthem. It's been recorded many times, including versions by Lead Belly, Mahalia Jackson, and Sonny Terry and Brownie McGhee.

Tupelo Honey was finished in early summer 1971 and reached the *Billboard* top 30. But as with *His Band and the Street Choir*, Morrison was not pleased with the final LP or the way his music was packaged. He also didn't like the large venues he was being asked to play. So while waiting for the album's release, he appeared that summer at a number of smaller California venues. He now seemed relaxed performing at clubs and halls that suited his style and allowed him to relate with the audience. One favourite new venue became the small folk and blues club where Janis Joplin's wake had been held. A tiny hangout for fewer than 200 people, The Lion's Share was Morrison's local joint on Red Hill Avenue in San Anselmo. It was a club he could ring up in the afternoon and book to play that evening, though someone else might have to be bumped down the bill. A recording exists of a great gig he played there in August, starting with a wonderful acoustic set taking in 'I Wanna Roo You', 'Sweet Thing', 'Street Choir', and 'Tupelo Honey'. When the band join him on the recording, the place is clearly rocking, and the climax of 'I've Been Working', 'Gloria' and 'Domino' shows Van in top form.

The next month, the set at San Francisco's Pacific High Studios – broadcast by KSAN – was varied and included several tracks from the new album: 'Wild Night', 'Moonshine Whiskey', 'You're My Woman', and 'Tupelo Honey'. The recording of the show is widely available. As at The

Lion's Share, 'Que Sera Sera' is resurrected from Morrison's apprentice days, and after asking his mother what he will be, he screams, 'You ain't nothing but a hound dog'. The band erupt into rock 'n' roll life for the Presley/Big Mama Thornton cover, and the concert switches between fast and slow for the next half a dozen songs. The night ends with the trio of singles from *His Band and The Street Choir* and a soulful cover of Sam Cooke's 'Bring It On Home To Me', before old fan favourite Louis Prima's 'Buona Sera (Signorina)' as a finale.

When Morrison could play an intimate venue, he was usually on fire. If he didn't feel that the music, the band, or the audience were working for him, he could end a show after 40 minutes, as he did in November 1971 at the Winterland or after just half a dozen numbers, as he did in March 1972 at the Berkeley Community Theatre. Morrison sang powerfully at the closing of the Fillmore West on 4 July 1971, even duetting with Lydia Pense and Linda Tillery on 'Rock Me Baby/My Babe' and 'I Found a Love', and he would have a much better time at the Winterland in the future, not least when he stole the show in 1976 performing on Thanksgiving Day with The Band at *The Last Waltz*.

It's been suggested that in 1971 Morrison was contemplating retiring from live performance and was only persuaded not to by playing small gigs around San Francisco that year – most notably at The Lion's Share, where he was even joined on stage by friends like Rick Danko, Jack Elliott, Bobby Neuwirth, and John Lee Hooker. Other San Francisco venues included Berkeley's New Orleans House, The Boarding House, the two Keystone clubs, and The Inn of the Beginning. There's a fascinating bootleg recording of Morrison at this last club in May 1971, performing a slow version of 'Beautiful Obsession' (which appeared coupled with the co-written 'Santa Fe' seven years later on *Wavelength*), referencing his oft-repeated 'train train' lyric, and showcasing the song's closing cowboy line.

In September 1971, Morrison sat in on a John Lee Hooker session at Wally Heider Studios. The resulting record *Never Get Out of These Blues Alive* notably features Morrison on the title track and also includes a version of 'T. B. Sheets'. Morrison contributed to other songs that were issued on that album's extended version, and on Hooker's subsequent 1973 album *Born in Mississippi, Raised in Tennessee* ('Going Down'). As noted in the opening chapter, the pair first met in 1964 in London, just before Them recorded Hooker's newly-released 'Don't Look Back'. And it's worth noting that – born in Mississippi – Hooker wrote and released a song called 'Tupelo Blues' in 1959. A striking contrast to Morrison's

'Tupelo Honey', it chronicles the city's great prewar flood.

Meanwhile, the *Tupelo Honey* reviews were mostly very positive. Jon Landau in *Rolling Stone*, Charlie Gillet in *Creem*, John Tobler in *ZigZag* and Richard Williams in *Melody Maker*, all praised the album's consistency, and admired the band's execution of Van's original compositions. Despite this, and even though it made the top 30 in the US, the album failed to chart in the UK. Warner Bros. considered the release another success, and it went on to sell well at the time but also as part of Van's back catalogue: at the time of writing, while *Moondance* stands at triple platinum, *Tupelo Honey* is the only other 1970s Morrison album to achieve gold certification in the US.

1972: Saint Dominic's Preview

Saint Dominic's Preview (1972)

Personnel:

Van Morrison: guitars, vocals

Ronnie Montrose: acoustic guitar; backing vocal ('Listen To The Lion')

Jules Broussard: tenor saxophone

Connie Kay: drums ('Listen To The Lion')

Lee Charlton: drums ('Almost Independence Day')

Ron Elliott: guitar ('Almost Independence Day')

Bill Church: bass

Rolf 'Boots' Houston: tenor saxophone ('Jackie Wilson Said'); backing vocal ('Listen To The Lion')

Mark Jordan: piano ('Listen To The Lion')

Bernie Krause: Moog synthesizer ('Almost Independence Day')

Rick Shlosser: drums

Gary Mallaber: drums, percussion, vibraphone

John McFee: steel guitar ('Saint Dominic's Preview')

Doug Messenger: guitars

Mark Naftalin: piano, Moog synthesizer

Pat O'Hara: trombone ('Saint Dominic's Preview', 'Gypsy')

Tom Salisbury: piano, organ

Jack Schroer: saxophone

Leroy Vinnegar: double bass ('Almost Independence Day')

Janet Planet, Ellen Schroer: backing vocals

Mark Springer: backing vocals ('Saint Dominic's Preview', 'Redwood Tree')

Producers: Ted Templeman, Van Morrison

All songs by Van Morrison

Recorded at Wally Heider Studios, Pacific High Studios, Columbia Studios, San Francisco, Summer 1971-Spring 1972

Release date: US: July 1972, UK: August 1972

Chart places: US: 15, UK: -

Running time: 41:34

Tracklisting: Side One: 1. 'Jackie Wilson Said (I'm In Heaven When You Smile)', 2. 'Gypsy', 3. 'I Will Be There', 4. 'Listen To The Lion'. Side Two: 1. 'Saint Dominic's Preview', 2. 'Redwood Tree', 3. 'Almost Independence Day'

The early months of 1972 began with more local gigs – mostly in small San Francisco venues but across California. The year's main touring then took place in May after the *Saint Dominic's Preview* sessions were complete. Venturing beyond California, Morrison played Seattle, Salem, Vancouver, Washington D.C., Philadelphia, Boulder, Albuquerque, Oklahoma, Pennsylvania, Boston and Providence, ending back at the Winterland in San Francisco. On 18 May, he played a particularly celebrated night at Carnegie Hall, which restored some of his enthusiasm for the road. At the gigs, he treated audiences to songs from the forthcoming album: 'Listen To The Lion', 'Saint Dominic's Preview', 'I Will Be There', and 'Jackie Wilson Said'. The well-received tour – still mainly in small venues like clubs, universities, and theatres – helped Van develop his material and expand upon the concept that inspired *His Band and the Street Choir*. This would culminate in the celebrated Caledonia Soul Orchestra of the following year. Meanwhile, on 22 June 1972, he again made the cover of *Rolling Stone* – this time staring down in an introspective pose, chosen and framed to imitate the *Astral Weeks* cover.

Straddling 1971 and 1972, *Saint Dominic's Preview* was made over many months at four different studios. It uses disparate musical styles and has a large cast of musicians. The saxophone is a major instrument here, but doesn't appear on either of the two-longest tracks. Ted Templeman and Morrison again co-produced, with Templeman responsible for keeping order in the studio and providing technical advice.

'Listen To The Lion' was already in the bag from the *Tupelo Honey* sessions at Columbia, featuring both Connie Kay and Ronnie Montrose, plus Gary Mallaber on percussion and vibes, pianist Mark Jordan and bassist Bill Church. Showcasing Morrison's leonine growling and rumblings, it was recorded in two takes, with 'Boots' Houston and Ronnie Montrose on backing vocals beside Van.

'Almost Independence Day' was recorded at Pacific High Studios in the autumn, not long after the September radio concert broadcast. For this track only, Ron Elliott played guitar, with bassist Leroy Vinnegar, drummer Lee Charlton, Bernie Krause on synth, and Mark Naftalin from The Paul Butterfield Blues Band on piano and Moog. Naftalin had been a part of the John Lee Hooker sessions Morrison joined at Wally Heider Studios.

In January 1972, 'Gypsy' and 'Jackie Wilson Said' were recorded with the touring band of Messenger, Schroer, Shlosser, Naftalin, and Church (Houston played saxophone on 'Jackie Wilson Said', but Jules Broussard substituted on 'Gypsy' with Pat O'Hara on trombone). The final three tracks were recorded back in April at Wally Heider Studios, with Mallaber on drums, Broussard on sax alongside Schroer, and Tom Salisbury replacing Naftalin on organ and piano. On 'Saint Dominic's Preview' Pat O'Hara plays trombone, and John McFee returns from *Tupelo Honey* to add steel guitar. Several engineers worked on the album, but all tracks were mixed by Templeman's long-term associate Donn Landee; except for 'Jackie Wilson Said', which was mixed by Bob Shumaker.

'Jackie Wilson Said (I'm in Heaven When You Smile)' is at least as good an opening track as 'Domino' or 'Wild Night'. It's another tribute – in particular to the 1957 track 'Reet Petite' (partly written by Berry Gordy, and inspired by Louis Jordan's 'Reet, Petite, And Gone'). The song was first demoed in January 1972 at Lee Michaels' studio in Mill Valley, south of San Rafael. For this early workout, Morrison and Doug Messenger played guitars, and Michaels played piano. The rest of the band were used on the final version recorded later that month at Pacific High. Working up the song beforehand seemed to help, and the players recorded it in one take. The track is striking for a number of effects: Morrison's opening refrain with handclaps, the gradual introduction of brass, strings, and percussion – beginning with the saxophones of Schroer and Houston – then the rest of the band; a drum roll ushering in the lyrics. Capping a near-perfect three-minute burst of joy and elation, Morrison scats at various points: seemingly part of the Wilson tribute. Otherwise, there's the sentiment of the chorus with Van declaring his loved one's smile takes him to paradise – a familiar Morrison trope, present, for example, on the demo he sent to Bert Berns back in 1967: 'I Love You (The Smile You Smile)'. That track was finally released on the 1991 compilation *Bang Masters*.

Several artists have covered 'Jackie Wilson Said'. Most well-known, Dexy's Midnight Runners' version reached number 5 in the UK in 1982. Wilson's 'Reet Petite' itself reached number 1 there when re-released in 1986, by which time Wilson was unable to benefit from the sales, having died two years earlier after a prolonged illness following a heart attack on stage in 1975. Morrison has said Wilson influenced his early vocal style, and Van's stage showmanship and singing, clearly indebted to James Brown, Bobby Bland, Ray Charles and other preacher-singers, may also owe something to Wilson.

Reaching only number 61, Van's 'Jackie Wilson Said' single was released in summer 1972 with a B-side of one of his rarest songs: 'You've Got The Power'. This is a Stax-influenced dance number with a soaring horn section and a jaunty swagger. The song's theme is love power – not the conflicted liberation of James Brown's 1960 song of the same name.

Owing something to the song's first attempt in summer 1969 as 'Set My Soul On Fire', 'You've Got The Power' has never been re-released, though it would've appeared on a proposed 1977 highlights compilation of Van's outtakes and rarities.

Like 'Gypsy Queen' before it, 'Gypsy' revives the lyric palette of 'Caravan' – the moon above, the campfire, the music, swaying underneath the stars with the one you love, and two guitars. But the music is very different from the earlier songs, using 4/4 and waltz time and backing vocals from two members of the Street Choir. There's also a declarative, driving horn opening. The ending is even more striking – backing vocalists Janet Planet and Ellen Schroer holding eerie final notes for several seconds: reverb sustaining the last syllable. The only side-one track with trombonist Pat O'Hara, 'Gypsy' was released as a single in January 1973, albeit in a shortened version.

With a piano and horn-led ten-second intro, 'I Will Be There' takes the album in another direction again. A lighthearted, amiable, laid-back song, it builds into a boisterous jump-blues track featuring honky-tonk piano and a sweet saxophone solo from Schroer. Morrison relies on simple lyric phrases to assert his loyalty whatever the circumstances, ending in the promise to join 'you' on a cruise with his razor, suitcase, toothbrush, overcoat, and 'my underwear'! Not to be confused with songs of the same title, this is a Morrison original, crying out to be covered. The best cover version, with a suitable big band, is by 20-year Morrison collaborator and saxophonist Pee Wee Ellis on Ellis's 1997 album *What You Like,* with Morrison guesting on vocals. Van has played the song in concert with different arrangements, and also recorded a faster horn-heavy version with Georgie Fame live at Ronnie Scott's (without an audience) to open the 1995 album *How Long has This Been Going On.*

Listeners in 1972 will have felt this album to so far be a set similar to *His Band and the Street Choir*: the funky soul opener, the gypsy song, and a 12-bar blues – a good run of tracks but one suggesting that Morrison's long, meditative songs were not going to return. At least three of the four remaining tracks intimate something different. 'Listen To The Lion' – a track as we know held over from *Tupelo Honey*, and first essayed back in 1969 – for most of its length seems like a blend of *Astral Weeks* with the expansive experimentation found in the 17-minute 'Caledonia Soul Music' demo from the *Street Choir* sessions, as it uses similar vocal, piano, and guitar figures. As significantly, 'Listen To The Lion' is a signature performance for Morrison's vocal abilities, his quest for spiritual enlightenment and his fascination with Caledonian heritage. In this last respect, it's similar to fellow Northern Irishman Seamus Heaney's 1975 collection *North* – a meditation on personal history, troubles, violent ancestry, and Viking roots. Like Heaney, Morrison never thought in the 1970s that his job was to be a spokesperson or that political situations could be reduced to simple side-taking.

The 'Listen To The Lion' lyric is in two distinct parts. The first is the soul-search for strength and courage in a time of crisis and sadness, culminating in the chorus three times. It starts by playing with the phrase 'All my love come tumbling down': most familiar from Wilson Pickett's 'In The Midnight Hour', though it didn't originate there (Morrison quotes the Pickett line at the end of 'Real, Real Gone' on *Enlightenment*). The second part can best be seen as the result of that search. It tells a journey in sound, with scattered images of the Viking longboats sailing from Denmark to Caledonia, and an intimation of Leif Eriksson's onward voyage to America. (The intriguing theme of an alternative America had the Vikings settled was used on Robert Calvert's Eno-produced concept album *Lucky Leif and the Longships* (1975).) This is also Van's genetic journey. Where Heaney uses a history of violence to explore the past behind the 'Troubles', Morrison's investigation of his history uses the flow of the oceans to suggest change; its toll being seen in terms of a flow of love and tears. Heaney's search is one mainly into the soil, using imagery such as the Mossbawn farmhouse where he grew up, the mythology of Antaeus, and the archaeological history of the Tollund Man. Whereas Morrison's is a search by sail – reflecting his own overseas journey to New York and California. Like his later exploration for the enigmatic Veedon Fleece, this is made personal through the quest for the lion, expressed through voice. 'Listen To The Lion' intimates how totemic Viking mast heads, dragons and lions, were used to protect the boat at sea and to embody the spirit or character of the vessel. In 2005, Morrison told *Uncut's* Nigel Williamson that the song 'came out of stuff I was reading at the time about the Phoenicians, who were one of the first seafaring races and came to Ireland way back. I read that they had lions carved on their boats, and that song came from that idea'. We can add to this the roots of the Morrison family as descendants of Viking settlers in Scotland, taking their ancestry from the paternal name Maurice: a derivation of the Latin Mauritius meaning 'dark'. Morrison has said 'Listen To The Lion' is one of his most personal songs, and one of the few he feels is actually about him.

Another consideration of Morrison's roots in relation to his present,

'Saint Dominic's Preview' became the title track of an album that was originally to be called 'Green'. The songs selected for the album were not decided in advance, and it's likely the earlier title reflected not only Van's Irish heritage but also an intention to record 'Bein' Green': a song that appears on the next album *Hard Nose the Highway*. 'Bein' Green' is a song best-known for its *Muppets* performance but widely covered, having recently been released by Lena Horne, and by Frank Sinatra on his 1971 album *Sinatra & Company*.

The released version of 'Saint Dominic's Preview' is notable for a number of elements. First, there's the artificial pronunciation of certain words and phrases – the distortion of 'wine', 'no regredior' instead of the 'no regrets' sung in previous takes, the play on 'empty shells/shelves', and the addition of 'cutting' to the phrase 'cross-country corner' as the words are written in Morrison's lyric book *Lit Up Inside*. Most of these were introduced when Morrison redid the vocal, feeling they needed more expressive interest.

Secondly, there's the title. Morrison told John Grissim for *Rolling Stone* in 1972: 'I'd been working on this song about the scene going down in Belfast, and I wasn't sure what I was writing. But anyway, the central image seemed to be this church called St. Dominic's, where people were gathering to pray or hear a mass for peace in Northern Ireland'. Then he read about a mass for peace in Belfast being held at a St. Dominic's church in San Francisco. This suggests that one important way of understanding the title is as a premonition: Morrison writing a song about a church called St. Dominic's seemed like a preview of the San Francisco event. To this day, there is indeed a St. Dominic's church in San Francisco, in a parish established in 1873 by the Dominican order. It's also fair to say the name is not uncommon and, for example, there's also a long-established St. Dominic's school on the Falls Road in Belfast. There are various allusions to the Troubles in Morrison's song, from 'orange' boxes to street marching, and the reference to 'flags and emblems' may well refer to the division emanating from the 1954 Flags and Emblems Act in Northern Ireland.

Thirdly, there are some of the musical effects – the organ part after the mention of Notre Dame, the pedal steel matching the reference to a 'Hank Williams railroad train' (e.g. 'The midnight train is whining low/I'm so lonesome I could cry'), Tom Salisbury's celebratory church arrangement, and Messenger's guitar overdub (at this point Messenger had been removed from the band but Morrison could find nobody else to play the part right).

Last, is the way Morrison weaves an arresting set of images, starting with him cleaning windows – as he used to do in Belfast – and singing songs about Edith Piaf. The introduction of Piaf's 'soul' leads to the mention of sombre voices emanating from Cathedral Notre-Dame. Whether what's heard from the Cathedral is a song or a mass (like at St. Dominic's) can suggest whether the listener hears the phrase as 'no regrets' (Piaf's 'Je ne regrette rien') or the Latin 'non regredior' (meaning 'go back' or 'return'). *Lit Up Inside* has the words as 'Ne Regrette Rien', which makes sense but is not what's sung on the album; 'non regredior' fits with the ending when Morrison sings 'Turned around' and 'Come back'.

Verse two shifts back to Morrison in San Francisco getting the song together and thinking about sitting with drummer Gary Mallaber, considering their respective long journeys home to Belfast and Buffalo. The much-debated Joyce reference here could be linked to Van's stream-of-consciousness lyric, but Morrison has denied this and Joyce is a common enough name in Ireland – and indeed America. The hugely suggestive 'blow the hoist' that follows 'Joyce' sounds like one of those occasions when the powerful internal rhyme drove the choice of words, suggesting that to rhyme with 'hoist' it may in fact, be 'joist' rather than 'Joyce' (like 'strain' and 'brain' or 'wet' and 'jet set'). By now, Morrison's associative method has meant any linear narrative evades the listener, leaving some wonderfully quotable phrases. The 'Preview' itself that follows is ambiguous and either looks beyond the present or gazes in dismay down on the scene: one of indifference to others' pain, no commitments, and talking behind doors. Here we get the lonesome whistle of the railroad songs lamenting cross-country train journeys, and the mention of symbols that oppress in a vision of disillusionment. These scattered fragments then give way to Morrison's disenchantment with his own circumstances now he's achieved renown as a musician – frustrations with the publicity game, news-hungry journalists, party people and hangers-on. As his career to date has made plain, this is not what Morrison thinks music should be about. Similarly, he sees falseness in the socialites of Manhattan and contrasts them with the freedom marchers out on the street.

The song ends by repeating how 'we' are watching Saint Dominic's revelation and then returns to the start with the closing reference to a 'soul meeting'. A gospel church effect comes through in several ways: the instrumentation, the repetition of the title against the soaring music, the impassioned vocal from the pulpit set against the chants from the three Street Choir singers, and the accusing phrases that lie behind the eye-strained vision of St. Dominic. If anything, it's a song about appearances and deceptions: common themes in Morrison's work. The song suggests that gazing out through the windows of the soul – whether via the cleaned panes of Belfast, the cathedral glass, the storey block or a 52nd Street apartment – provides a different point of view or a preview of a similar prospect. If further historical context for St. Dominic's vision is wanted, a good place to start is Benozzo Gozzoli's Renaissance painting 'Vision of St. Dominic and Meeting of St. Francis and St. Dominic'. The painting concerns a premonition of destruction to be visited on the world and the uniting of the two saints, who each had such a vision, and supposedly vowed to work together to avert God's wrath. Such background is presumably coincidental but suggests a connection with San Francisco, which was not only Morrison's home at this point but was the main setting for all of side two's songs.

'Redwood Tree' brings together images of childhood with the old, tall venerable redwoods near Morrison's house in Marin County. We might therefore note that as a schoolboy, Van had a pet dog, and even thought of becoming a vet. I've mentioned the song's echo of 'Come Running', but its nostalgic lyric about a transformative experience in nature is also similar to 'And It Stoned Me', if with a sense of loss and learning rather than bliss. The song may be seen as a parable or fable, but its meaning is open-ended, suggesting enlightenment and mystery. It's one of the few Morrison songs that seem to follow a storyline, whereas most of his lyrics are built around images, phrases, word sounds, and associations. In October 1972, a different mix of 'Redwood Tree' was released as the album's second single, with 'Saint Dominic's Preview' or 'Jackie Wilson Said' on the flipside in different territories, peaking just inside the US top 100.

The hypnotic 'Almost Independence Day' is a meditation that starts with Morrison humming as he almost appears to search for the song on his guitar. It's similar in approach to The Rolling Stones' 'Moonlight Mile' (1971), but the closest echo is found in the opening of Pink Floyd's 'Wish You Were Here' (1975), which is easily confused with Morrison's song. After 45 seconds, the 'Almost Independence Day' intro stops, and the main theme begins with the rest of the band: most notably Ron Elliott on acoustic guitar. This is shortly before the Moog synthesizer foghorn sound washes over the listener, bringing to mind 'Into The Mystic'. With Morrison in San Francisco, the lyric starts to the north with voices 'calling from Oregon', suggesting another journey to parallel 'Listen To The Lion', though this time it's further west across the Pacific towards China. The song's journey is to San Francisco to buy some 'Hong Kong silver' from Chinatown, while the bay sights and sounds create an inner journey for the singer. Morrison has said that the line at the start about hearing voices refers to a ghost call that he received when the operator failed to connect him with a musician phoning from up the coast. This odd occurrence feeds into the experience of a cool night on the town, seeing the lights of boats way out in the harbour and hearing the distant sound of fireworks along the bay on the 4th of July; the explosions echoing up and down the bay, and people shouting up and down the line. This becomes a song about spiritual yearning through sensory perception; about distant hearing, seeing, and feeling, while the idea of something *nearly* happening fuels the title's expectation and the apprehension of far-away movement in the stillness and darkness: someone trying to connect long-distance, faintly heard along the line.

Besides the mantric words – often intoned in syllables simultaneously picked on guitar – Naftalin's low Moog synthesizer wave (suggesting harbour sounds (boats, foghorns)) defines the music's overwhelming rolling up-and-down feel, with a cycle of sonic swirls similar in meditative impact to some of the later sections of 'Madame George'. Like that song and later moodscapes like 'When Heart Is Open' on *Common One*, 'Almost Independence Day' *almost* invites the listener to fall into a trance. The other feature is the guitars of Morrison and Elliott: as though imitating the echoing voices trying to communicate up and down the telephone line. The song closes with a return to the humming, alongside 12-string guitar, before giving way to Naftalin's Moog foghorn, which itself fades into the distance, leaving silence once more. At the end of recording the track, Morrison asked Krause to add a high Moog part to convey the impression of Chinatown dragons and fireworks.

No live recordings of 'Almost Independence Day' seem to exist. This is unlike 'Wonderful Remark', an almost equally-long version of which was recorded around this time. According to *The Philosopher's Stone* liner notes, this recording of 'Wonderful Remark' took place in 1973 at the Church in San Anselmo, but according to some, it might've been during the 1972 *Saint Dominic's Preview* sessions. Morrison has said the song was effectively about his own predicament at the turn of the 1970s as an artist producing idealistic music while struggling to make ends meet. Many outtakes were taped amid the final album recordings, including more covers – Hooker's 'Boogie Chillen' (recorded in 2000 for *You Win Again* with Linda Gail Lewis), Ray Charles' 'Drown In My Own Tears', and

The Everly Brothers' 'Let it Be Me', which Morrison had been performing in concert, as we noted in the last chapter.

Michael Maggid was retained from *Tupelo Honey* to do the cover photography. In keeping with the album title, the cover was shot locally at the San Francisco Theological Seminary on the steps leading to the Montgomery Chapel door. The back cover was shot at Maggid's workplace in San Rafael.

Saint Dominic's Preview was Morrison's first top-20 album in the US, and his highest-placed *Billboard* LP of the 1970s: number 15. Despite increased Warner Bros. advertising, the record didn't chart in the UK, where Morrison had yet to tour. The album garnered positive reviews and was generally seen as his best collection since *Moondance*.

Morrison closed out 1972 with a new 16-track recording studio built onto the back of his house in Fairfax; he called it Caledonia Studio. Not finished until late summer, it was a useful space for rehearsals earlier in the year but was only put to serious use from August, capturing new compositions and a few songs he knew from his youth. These became outtakes – including the John Henry-like work song 'Take This Hammer', which Morrison has played live and later sang on Mitch Woods' 2017 album *Friends Along the Way*. Meanwhile, Janet Planet departed the scene and appeared on no more albums. Old band members Jef Labes and John Platania flew out on several occasions to work on fresh songs, and a tour was planned for the Caledonia Soul Orchestra.

The new studio allowed a more free and easy recording process, and all of the next album *Hard Nose the Highway,* was recorded before the year's end, even though the LP wasn't released until the following August, a year after the first tracks were committed to tape. With time on his hands and studio space of his own in which to record, Morrison was entering one of the most creative periods of his career, and all despite occasional fear of writer's block, which had no discernible effect on his output for another couple of years.

1973: Hard Nose the Highway

Hard Nose the Highway (1973)

Personnel:

Van Morrison: acoustic guitar, vocals, arrangements

Rick Shlosser: drums

David Hayes: bass

John Platania: guitar

Jules Broussard: flute, tenor saxophone

Bill Atwood: trumpet

Marty David: bass ('Bein' Green', 'Wild Children')

Jackie DeShannon: backing vocals ('Warm Love', 'Hard Nose The Highway')

Joe Ellis: trumpet ('Hard Nose The Highway', 'Bein' Green')

Theresa 'Terry' Adams: cello

Nancy Ellis: viola

Michael Gerling, Zaven Melikian, Nathan Rubin, John Tenney: violin

Jef Labes: piano, keyboards, string arrangements

Gary Mallaber: vibraphone, drums

Jack Schroer: saxophone; brass arrangements

Oakland Symphony Chamber Chorus: vocals ('Snow In San Anselmo')

Producer: Van Morrison

All songs by Van Morrison except where stated

Recorded at Caledonia Studio, Fairfax, August and October 1972

Release date: US: August 1973, UK: July 1973

Chart places: US: 27, UK: 22

Running time: 43:12

Tracklisting: Side One: 1. 'Snow In San Anselmo', 2. 'Warm Love', 3. 'Hard Nose The Highway', 4. 'Wild Children', 5. 'The Great Deception'. Side Two: 1. 'Bein' Green' (Joe Raposo), 2. 'Autumn Song', 3. 'Purple Heather' (Trad.)

Though only one album was released in each of the years, late 1972 through to the end of 1973 constitute one of Morrison's most-fertile musical periods. Freedom to record and a familiar set of musicians created an environment in which Van could write and record much more easily than ever.

The first album that emerged from the new studio was an excellent though sometimes under-appreciated follow-up to *Saint Dominic's Preview*, which itself followed two albums Morrison thought were marred by compromise and interference.

One of the problems with the reputation of *Hard Nose the Highway* is simply that a lot of great material remained behind in the vaults. There were too many good songs and potential projects for one disc to capture the variety of Morrison's output; one of his strengths is the diversity of his musical interests, but to assemble a set of disparate songs that people find coherent despite the breadth of styles, as on *Saint Dominic's Preview*, is no easy feat. By the time of the release of *The Philosopher's Stone* in 1998, it was clear that, among other prime material, a superb set of nine songs was in the can that could've been an album in 1973. If released at the time, these songs probably would've been considered another first-class Morrison record, whether alongside *Hard Nose the Highway* or as the second disc of a double LP.

If we take these tracks from *The Philosopher's Stone* in sequence, they start with the sublime 'Not Supposed To Break Down'. Its four players (Morrison: acoustic guitar, Shaar: drums, Hayes: bass, Labes: piano) are also the core musicians across most of the rest of the songs. The title draws on the Robert Johnson/Sonny Boy Williamson blues staple 'Stop Breaking Down', but Morrison's lyric has a different focus – one which would've exactly suited the thematic intent of *Hard Nose the Highway*. Morrison said that the album was meant to be about the difficulty of working in the music business, and 'Not Supposed To Break Down' pinpoints the mental strain for an artist, or any feeling human being, living in the contemporary world, much like the track 'The Great Deception' discussed below. Illustrating how *The Philosopher's Stone* contains some of Morrison's finest material, 'Not Supposed To Break Down' is a classic recording of vocal beauty and deep feeling caught between disillusionment, determination, stoicism and cynicism.

The next song, 'Laughing In The Wind', is in complete contrast and was performed live a few times in 1973 (unlike 'Not Supposed To Break Down'). It features American singer-songwriter Jackie DeShannon on backing vocals and has the standard *Hard Nose the Highway* personnel, but with Shlosser on drums and the Schroer and Broussard horn section. Another carefree love song, its lyric draws on Morrison's archetypal springtime trope, including the assurance that there's 'No need to wonder why'.

Supposedly linked to a possible 1973 film project, 'Madame Joy' is among Morrison's best songs; a kind of sequel to 'Madame George', but in no way resembling it. Celebrating another iconic figure walking down the street, the song's splendour rests on its melody, the sweet, high-pitched singing, Broussard's flute, Schroer's sax, and Platania's distinctive, plaintive electric guitar-playing: one of the joys of Morrison's band in this period. For this song, Mallaber is on drums.

'Contemplation Rose' has the core quartet of players for an update on 'Spanish Rose' with a tune resembling 'Snow In San Anselmo'. Another piano-based song like 'Not Supposed To Break Down', 'Contemplation Rose' opens with a sweet Puerto Rican nursery rhyme couplet before the lyric focuses on a church in Spanish Harlem housing the contemplated rose. Preceding 'Kingdom Hall' by a few years, it references the Jehovah's Witnesses magazines *Watchtower* and *Awake!*, but seems to reject them for the mystic rose tradition representing divine love, and the more earthly romantic and carnal imagery of the rose behind Jerry Leiber's lyric for 'Spanish Harlem'.

'Don't Worry About Tomorrow' is a loping, largely instrumental blues, introduced by some of Morrison's most sustained and prominent harmonica-playing, and featuring Labes experimenting on piano from about halfway through, just before the lyric kicks in.

'Try For Sleep' is co-written by John Platania and is again sweetly sung in Morrison's highest register. Featuring Bill Atwood's cool, rasping trumpet complemented by Mark Jordan's piano phrasing, it opens with the Faron Young reference 'It's Four o'clock in the morning', and takes its theme from Ray Charles' 'Lonely Avenue' (the song Morrison covered in 1993 on *Too Long in Exile*, and with which he started the medley that contains 'Try For Sleep' on the 1994 live album *A Night in San Francisco*). The lyric contains an early reference to the idea of 'pushin' the river', and the song was known earlier as 'Family Affair', with nods to the Sly Stone song of that name. Clocking in at over six minutes, 'Try For Sleep' is a languid study in soul/jazz dynamics that would electrify any venue, though Morrison only performed it live a few times in the 1970s.

'Lover's Prayer' has a simple chorus consisting of the repeated word 'Lord' as an invocation to introduce the prayer to be with the beloved. Another great song, 'Drumshanbo Hustle' was named after Morrison's 1964 experience with a showband trying to find a County Leitrim concert venue. It melds several bad recording contract situations in which he found himself in the 1960s, with his feelings about attempts to exploit and threaten him after Bert Berns' death. It's therefore worth remembering that *T. B. Sheets* – the next batch of songs from the New York sessions with Berns – was issued in 1973 after a court battle. Beginning with a familiar blues image of appearing before 'the judge', 'Drumshanbo Hustle' must be one of very few songs with a repeated refrain about puking up your guts. The song was debuted live at Dublin's RTE studio in November.

Finally, in the *The Philosopher's Stone* collection of songs from the *Hard Nose the Highway* sessions (though the compilation oddly attributes it to 1976), is 'There There Child' – a song performed live only in mid-1973; its live version included on *It's Too Late to Stop Now Vol III*. Featuring the Caledonia Soul Orchestra core band of Hayes, Shaar, Platania, and Labes, this flight of imagination is a comforting lullaby about winging over the white cliffs of Dover, with a similar sentiment to the 1941 song by Burton and Kent made famous by Vera Lynn. Platania has a writing credit on 'There There Child', which was to be included with 'Try For Sleep' and 'Laughing In The Wind' on the 14-track collection of unreleased tracks that Warner Bros. prepared in 1977 when they needed a follow-up to *Veedon Fleece.* In the end, it was decided an album of new material would be preferable.

So, these tracks took 25 years to be officially released and the reasons for them languishing in the vault are both artistic and commercial. As mentioned above, it is often thought the tracks on an album need to cohere into a whole, so choices have to be made in the moment, sometimes hastily. Also, Warner Bros. appear to have wanted to limit the amount of 'product' on the shop shelves, forcing Morrison to restrict his musical output at a time when he was most prolific.

Another fine and substantial recording (of well over six minutes) from the *Hard Nose the Highway* sessions – the mellow acoustic-guitar driven 'Tell Me (All About Your love)' – surprisingly appeared at the turn of the millennium on one of the alternative CD releases of the single 'Back On Top' (along with the minor track 'Sax Instrumental No.1'), listed as from 1975.

Other outtakes yet to see the light of day were recorded at this time, and there are still riches in the studio vaults that could be profitably mined. But it was decided that the focus, or concept, for the new album to be issued in 1973 was to be the contrast between two sets of experiences. The local country, woodland, and greenery around Marin County inspired one suite of gentle songs, harnessed together on side two. But the overriding theme was expressed in a preceding set of five songs, encapsulated in the title *Hard Nose the Highway*. Side one focuses on life's harsh realities, with lyrics of change and becoming, about life in San Anselmo, love, touring, the postwar generation, and the music business. These are followed on side two by the three lighter tracks, sometimes called 'leaf' songs, which are about being and deal far more with the seasons, inner life, and the individual's relationships with nature.

Like the shelved songs discussed above, *Hard Nose the Highway* was recorded at Van's 8-track Caledonia Studio. All tracks were cut in the latter months of 1972. One of the five engineers who worked on *Moondance* – Neil Schwartz, mixed the album and was also sole engineer at the sessions in late August when the first tracks were recorded – 'Bein' Green', 'Purple Heather', 'Wild Children', 'Snow In San Anselmo', and 'The Great Deception'. Jim Stern joined Schwartz in October for 'Autumn Song', 'Warm Love' and 'Hard Nose The Highway'.

Morrison was now personally able to assemble a team of players with whom he wanted to work. And the gathered musicians would go on to shape the concert band with which he is probably still most often associated. Platania and Labes were back on board, and Morrison found an excellent local bassist in David Hayes, with Marty David featuring on just two tracks: 'Bein' Green' and 'Wild Children'. Drums were shared between Mallaber and Shlosser, though Dahaud Shaar was soon to return for gigs. Mallaber also played vibes. Horns and flute were supplied by Schroer, Broussard, Joseph Ellis and Bill Atwood. But the real new addition was the array of string players: Nancy Ellis on viola, Terry Adams on cello, Nathan Rubin, John Tenney, Michael Gerling and Zaven Melikian on violins. String arrangements were by Labes, and brass by Schroer, with Morrison also providing a guiding hand, most obviously on 'Purple Heather'. Jackie DeShannon appeared on backing vocals (strikingly on 'Warm Love' but also on 'Hard Nose the Highway'), while the Oakland Symphony Chamber Chorus were enlisted for the atmospheric and portentous first track, 'Snow In San Anselmo'.

Hard Nose the Highway has no R&B, 12-bar blues, or gypsy songs. It can be seen as a waypoint between the two critically-approved milestones of *Saint Dominic's Preview* and *Veedon Fleece*. Morrison wanted to release a double album, and this would've resulted from a different conceptual approach. However, the album as released has its own coherence and contains some great music, though it is unlike any other Morrison LP. It reflects the work of the burgeoning Caledonia Soul Orchestra and showcases the arrangement approach that Morrison, Labes, and Schroer explored before hitting the road.

Opener 'Snow In San Anselmo' is another example of the experimental departures Morrison had unveiled on *Saint Dominic's Preview*. It also shows the freedom afforded by the new recording situation. The regular

Van on stage in 1974, the *annus mirabilis* of his phenomenal early run of stellar album releases. (*Alamy*)

Left: The cover photograph used for the 1966 *Them Again* album. (*Decca*)

Right: Recorded at Them's first studio session, Van's rock classic *Gloria* was inducted into the Grammy Hall of Fame in 1999.

Left: In posture and attitude, the unsmiling Them presented themselves as 'angry young men' in the mould of the working-class writers of the 1950s.

Right: Van on stage at the Filmore East in 1970.

Left: The gig featured a band of Jef Labes, John Klingberg, Gary Mallaber, John Platania, Jack Schroer and Collin Tilton.

Right: Caught one more time on the avenue of trees.

Left: Joel Brodsky took the iconic *Astral Weeks* photo the year after he'd shot the most famous 'Young Lion' photo of Van's namesake Jim Morrison. (*Warner Bros*)

Right: Janet Planet's liner notes for *Moondance* begin 'Once upon a time, there lived a very young man who was, as they say, gifted'. (*Warner Bros*)

Left: On the back cover of *Moondance*, the beard is gone, adding to the sense that Morrison's image was as yet far from agreed upon. (*Warner Bros*)

Right: Janet Planet designed the album cover for *His Band and the Street Choir* using a photo of Van in a kaftan he had bought in Woodstock. (*Warner Bros*)

VAN MORRISON HIS BAND AND THE STREET CHOIR

VAN MORRISON
HIS BAND AND THE STREET CHOIR

DOMINO
CRAZY FACE
GIVE ME A KISS
I'VE BEEN WORKING
CALL ME UP IN DREAMLAND
I'LL BE YOUR LOVER, TOO

BLUE MONEY
VIRGO CLOWNS
GYPSY QUEEN
SWEET JANNIE
IF I EVER NEEDED SOMEONE
STREET CHOIR

Left: Band members were (left to right) Alan Hand, Larry Goldsmith, Keith Johnson, Dahaud Shaar, John Klingberg and Jack Schroer. (*Warner Bros*)

Van Morrison

Tupelo Honey

Right: Reviews of *Tupelo Honey* on release were extremely positive: 'the perfect album' (Dave Marsh), 'the real thing' (John Tobler) and 'perfectly integrated' (Jon Landau). (*Warner Bros*)

Left: Morrison was joined by John Platania and David Hayes for his *Old Grey Whistle Test* interview with Bob Harris.

Right: In 1976, Platania formed the LA band Giants, which included Ron Elliott, who plays on 'Almost Independence Day' and Bruce Gary, who went on to be the drummer in The Knack.

Left: When asked about future plans, Van tells Harris he's going to read some scripts and get into movie scores.

Right: Van's rendition of 'Brown Eyed Girl' with the Caledonia Soul Orchestra was featured in the Live at the Rainbow broadcast from July 1973.

Left: The track was left off the original *It's Too Late to Stop Now* release in 1974, as were the filmed recordings of 'Moonshine Whiskey' and 'Moondance'.

Right: The Rainbow concert video was finally released in 2016 with the multi-disc set *It's Too Late to Stop Now Volumes II, II* and *IV* on Exile Productions.

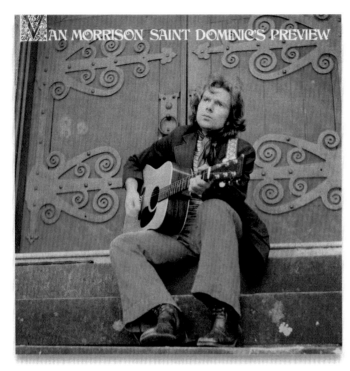

Left: Many have noticed the rip in Morrison's jeans on the cover of *St Dominic's Preview*. (*Warner Bros*)

Right: Rob Springett designed the cover art of *Hard Nose the Highway* after a conversation with Morrison about its themes and songs. (*Warner Bros*)

Right: Morrison directed the Caledonia Soul Orchestra with hand gestures during the *It's Too Late to Stop Now* tour. (*Warner Bros*)

Left: Tom Collins photographed Van at the Sutton Castle Hotel, a converted mansion overlooking Dublin Bay, for the cover of *Veedon Fleece*. (*Warner Bros*)

Left: A rare appearance in 1976, at the Winterland for *The Last Waltz* with The Band.

Right: Robbie Robertson immortalizes Morrison as Van the Man as he high-kicks off the stage at the end of 'Moondance'.

Left: 'I Shall be Released' has Morrison on stage with Dylan for the first time. Dr. John is also there at *The Last Waltz*, far left.

Right: Morrison back at Montreux in 1980.

Left: John Platania, Pee Wee Ellis, and Mark Isham also have their moments to shine during the show.

Right: 'IOU Angel'. Van signs off at Montreux with 'Angeliou' as the final song.

Left: From distraction to a half-smile as the camera gets closer to illustrate *A Period of Transition*. (*Warner Bros*)

Right: *Wavelength* would be Morrison's last album for Warner Bros. (*Warner Bros*)

Right: Morrison's last album of the 1970s was a return to top form, with Robert Christgau in *The Village Voice* declaring *Into the Music* his best album since *Moondance*. (*Polydor*)

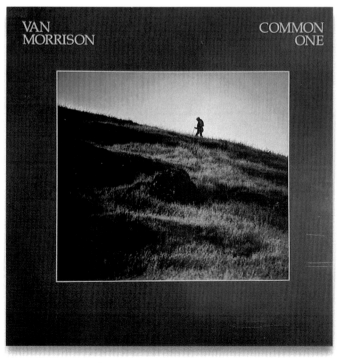

Left: *Common One* illustrated a new direction, drawing on free jazz, but critics didn't understand, at least until Lester Bangs re-evaluated it as 'holy music' in 1982. (*Mercury/ Warner/Polydor*)

Left: 'Brown Eyed Girl' was originally titled 'Brown Skinned Girl'. The reasons for the change are debated, but Van says it was just a mistake.

Right: 'Crazy Love'. Van later sang a duet of the song with Bob Dylan in the 1991 film *One Irish Rover*.

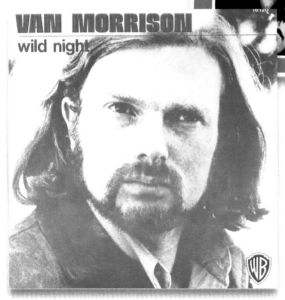

Left: 'Wild Night' was a 1971 hit in the USA and Canada.

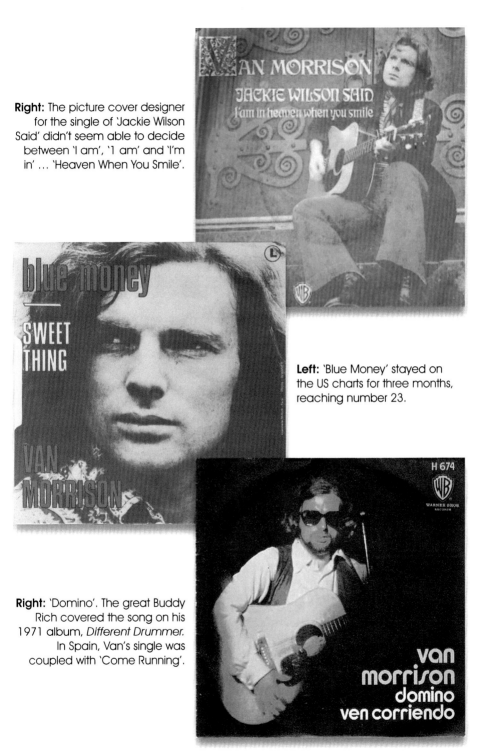

Right: The picture cover designer for the single of 'Jackie Wilson Said' didn't seem able to decide between 'I am', 'I am' and 'I'm in' … 'Heaven When You Smile'.

Left: 'Blue Money' stayed on the US charts for three months, reaching number 23.

Right: 'Domino'. The great Buddy Rich covered the song on his 1971 album, *Different Drummer.* In Spain, Van's single was coupled with 'Come Running'.

Left: Live recordings of various quality have made it on to CD, but some releases at least do show Morrison at his peak.

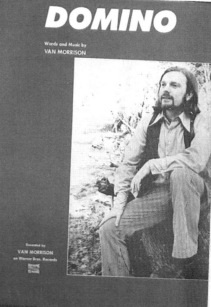

Right: Reaching number nine, 'Domino' is Morrison's highest-charting single in the US, surpassing 'Brown Eyed Girl' by one place.

Left: 'Bright Side of the Road' was Van's only single to chart in the UK in the 1970s, reaching number 63.

band members were surprised to enter Caledonia Studio one day to find the space dominated by the Oakland Symphony Chamber Chorus. Their effect on the album is immediate. Accompanied only by Labes' piano, the choir's slightly eerie harmonies seem to take their cue from the sustained ending note of 'Gypsy' on *Saint Dominic's Preview* – creating an atmosphere that complements the lyrics' emphasis on the extraordinary appearance of snowfall in the town. Sometimes through juxtaposition, Schroer's and Labes' arrangements underline the song's events – whether it be the band quickening after mention of the radio station or the clear, crisp guitar notes accompanying Morrison's ice description. The song is itself a glacial mini-opera, and the arrangements are a follow-on from 'Saint Dominic's Preview', uniting strings, horns, and voices to match the mood of the story. Morrison says the song describes his experiences one night. But set out as a lyric, the images inevitably seem to accumulate some no-doubt unintended meaning. The snow appears like Dylan's hard rain, as a judgement coming to clean the town of its gangs, drugs, and sleaze: all obliquely mentioned. The reference to the radio station playing 'soft and low', also seems to echo Dylan's 'The country music station plays soft' from 'Visions Of Johanna'. 'Snow In San Anselmo' shifts from a light jazz feel, to a sped-up horn-led frenzy in between the verses, as the choir repeats closing lines of Morrison's A/B/C/B rhymes.

Melodic concert favourite 'Warm Love' praises the pervasive glow of an enveloping happiness. To underline the idea of omnipresence, the song gives four pictures of bliss: in the garden, in dressing-up, in the country sun, and drying off by the fire after returning from the beach in the rain. Morrison sings in a high register, as he had on several previous love songs. Jackie DeShannon accompanies him on backing vocals – not in a duet but indicating how the song could work well sung that way. The highlight for many is Broussard's smooth, affecting and lyrical flute-playing, but it wasn't enough to find 'Warm Love' a place in the US or UK charts when released as a single.

The album's title track references tough times for Morrison in Marin County (at the Grateful Dead's place), but worse in Belfast and Boston. The coda name-checks Bobby Bland's 1957 single 'Further On Up The Road'. It also quotes 'These Dreams Of You' from *Moondance*, when Morrison sings towards the end about paying your dues north of the border. The song's theme is the hard life in the music business and especially on tour. This is contrasted with the ideal of Sinatra laying down a first take against a Nelson Riddle orchestra arrangement, then heading off, not on the road but on vacation. Frank Sinatra was in some ways a model artist and singer for Morrison, and what Riddle once said to Robin Douglas-Home of Sinatra could also be said to apply to Morrison: 'In working out arrangements for Frank, I suppose I stuck to two main rules. First, find the peak of the song and build the whole arrangement to that peak, pacing it as he paces himself vocally. Second, when he's moving, get the hell out of the way.... After all, what arranger in the world would try to fight against Sinatra's voice? Give the singer room to breathe'.

The next song, 'Wild Children', is about growing up with American heroes after World War II. It commemorates a generation who wanted change and who rebelled against their parents. Like the previous track's homage to the mid-1950s Sinatra albums, 'Wild Children' paints a romantic and bittersweet picture of the transatlantic icons and dramatic figures of Morrison's adolescence, who inspired him in his formative years. A sublime, romantic composition, the song found its shimmering peak on the road and is best appreciated on the live album *It's Too Late to Stop Now*.

Van's lyric for 'Wild Children' about youthful inspiration picks out four key countercultural postwar figures, James Dean, Marlon Brando, Rod Steiger, and Tennessee Williams. The song locates the fountainhead as Tennessee Williams – whose *A Streetcar Named Desire* was first performed on Broadway in 1947 and starred Marlon Brando in his breakthrough role. The missing person who best holds the quartet together is probably Elia Kazan – the groundbreaking social-issues theatre and film director who made three of the 1950s most iconic movies: the adaptation of his own pioneering production *A Streetcar Named Desire,* with Brando, *On the Waterfront* (1954) with Rod Steiger and Brando playing brothers, and James Dean's film debut *East of Eden*. Kazan discovered both Brando and Dean, and the latter was enamoured with the older actor. Dean and Steiger had acted together on TV in the early-1950s and were close friends. Appealing to Morrison's sensibilities, all three were method actors promoting naturalistic authenticity and emotional truth, and had studied at New York's famous Actor's Studio, which Kazan co-founded. If we want to ask where the album's other icon, Sinatra, connects, it's a fascinating fact that he was at one point contracted to play Brando's role in *On the Waterfront*, and indeed Sinatra sued for breach of contract when the younger actor was used. The two appeared together in *Guys and Dolls* – which hit cinemas at the start of November 1955: exactly one week after Dean's posthumously-released *Rebel Without a Cause*. 'Wild Children' pinpoints Dean's death, in a California car accident on 30 September 1955, as a kind of watershed – a pivotal moment in the mourning of a postwar generation, before Buddy Holly's death in 1959, or the 1963 assassination of John F. Kennedy. Three four-line verses make up the entire lyric – their sequence in the second half changed to end with the beginning verse, but this time referring not to 'war children' (looking back), but to 'wild children', looking forward to the rebellious attitudes adopted by the generation who took Brando and Dean as their heroes. Dean's starring role in *Rebel Without a Cause* (1955) came after Brando had starred as the leader of the Black Rebels Motorcycle Club in 'The Wild One' (1953). In response, that year to the emergence of such new 'wild children', FBI Director J. Edgar Hoover, warned of 'an appalling increase in the number of crimes that will be committed by teenagers in the years ahead'.

It's back to the present on the next song, 'The Great Deception', in which a 'great Hollywood motion picture actor' is now just a drunk in the gutter, and everyone rips you off in 'love city'. John Platania – whose guitar-playing is the highlight – has said that most of the words were written on the spot. As a lyric drawing on Morrison's resentment at the turn of the decade when he was struggling to live above the bread line, it berates all those – from inauthentic revolutionaries to the press – who make money on the back of artists and who pedal duplicity, whether selling peace and love, drugs and fantasy, or publicity and scandal. The origin of the lyric was a letter Van received from a would-be freedom fighter asking for a big donation to the cause. Morrison's first clear early-1970s sideswipe at a world of hustlers, the lyric picks up on some earlier lines: particularly the disillusionment expressed at the close of 'Saint Dominic's Preview'. The title 'The Great Deception' seems to play on the term 'The Great Depression', which referred to the social and economic downturn of the 1930s, and Morrison's picture of 1970s realities suggests an era of cultural duplicity after the authenticity of his 1950s heroes cited in 'Wild Children'.

Side one's blend of nostalgia for better times and despair at the present is balanced by side two's lightness and space. 'Bein' Green' is a transition: the album's last song of spring. The lyric takes the ordinary and turns it into affirmation, perceiving strength and everyday splendour through a revelation, delivered via a soaring vocal. Though Morrison didn't write 'Bein' Green' – his first cover on a Warner Bros. album – its resilient and ultimately celebratory message chimes with his own philosophy: the variations on 'wonder why' that appear in his lyrics from 'Beside You'

(*Astral Weeks*) to 'Summertime in England' on *Common One* (1980). The hymn to nature's unassuming beauty on 'Bein' Green' leads to the lightness of the two closing autumnal songs. And 'Bein' Green' is also a great vocal performance: perhaps a sly nod to the fact that Sinatra had just recorded the song himself, as noted in the last chapter. 'Bein' Green' was released as a single but, like 'Warm Love', it didn't chart in the UK or US.

Stephen Holden's September 1973 *Rolling Stone* review – though at odds with some other critics – found much to admire on side two and is worth quoting:

> As was the case in *St. Dominic's Preview*, the second side of the album turns out to be better than the first. The ten-minute 'Autumn Song' demonstrates anew Van's gift at creating extended meditations that accumulate emotional power as they unfold in modified, impressionistic streams of consciousness … evoking – as few contemporary composers have – the ineffable joys of daily life in attunement to a pleasant environment. The music is laid-back and sparkling, highlighted by the lovely pianism of Jef Labes, and the doubled guitars of Van and John Platania.

Like 'Bein' Green', 'Autumn Song' could've been covered by Sinatra very effectively, and it surely invokes the spirit of Nat King Cole in the mention of roasting chestnuts: here before Halloween rather than Christmas. Holden goes on:

> 'Autumn Song' is sandwiched between two other mellow delights. Joe Raposo's 'Green' [sic] is an enchanting bit of poetic whimsy set in rock-&-roll triplets, and featuring a lusty horn break that segues into shivering strings. The album closes with Van's beautiful arrangement of the traditional 'Purple Heather', which he has transformed into an ethereal 'Astral Weeks' reverie that fades out on his inimitable rock scat-singing … 'Da da da, Da da da, Da da da' echoed between voice and piano, with glissando strings hovering overhead.

Arranged by Morrison, 'Purple Heather' is a version of the 1950s song 'Wild Mountain Thyme' – adapted by Belfast-born Francis McPeake from the poet Robert Tannahill's much older Scottish song 'The Braes Of Balquhidder'. Morrison had heard the McPeakes play it at a Belfast party, but it was also a song his mother sung. In Morrison's rendition, it's another autumn song, with leaves turning after the summertime has gone. One of several often-overlooked gems on the album, 'Purple Heather' is a string-led *tour de force*. The opening guitar is soon eclipsed by Jef Labes' scaling piano, which builds to a crescendo before eventually giving centre stage to beautiful swirling violins. It's a tower of sound, built to deliver on the mountain-greenery promises of 'Bein' Green', though it fades all too soon just before the six-minute mark, with the string section still in full flow. This rendition is magisterial, even if it's often listed as just another of the myriad interpretations by artists from Dylan (at the Isle of Wight) to The Byrds and Rod Stewart. A beautiful live version with the Caledonia Soul Orchestra is included on the 2016 *It's Too Late To Stop Now* multi-CD set.

As mentioned earlier, Jackie DeShannon sang on the album and gigged a little with Morrison in 1973. The pair collaborated more extensively at Caledonia Studio in April after *Hard Nose the Highway* had been recorded. On her 1972 album *Jackie*, she had already covered Morrison's 'I Wanna Roo You', which was also the B-side of her single 'Paradise' that year. Curiously, for her 1971 Capitol Records album *Songs*, she'd recorded 'Down By The Riverside' at the same time Morrison had considered the song for his mooted country covers album. She also recorded a country/gospel version of 'And It Stoned Me' for Capitol, but it remained unreleased for decades, eventually appearing on the *Songs* reissue.

In April 1973, Morrison wrote, produced, and performed on 'Sweet Sixteen': a catchy, swinging DeShannon pop single released in June. They also co-wrote 'Santa Fe', which Morrison recorded for *Wavelength* (1978). Their other recordings together from this time were only released in 2003 on the *Jackie... Plus* expanded version. These include a version of 'Flamingos Fly' (which Morrison recorded for *A Period of Transition*), and his little-known 'The Wonder Of You' with Morrison on backing vocals. During the *Hard Nose the Highway* sessions, he also recorded Christine McVie's 'Spare Me A Little (Of Your Love)' (from Fleetwood Mac's *Bare Trees*), featuring DeShannon on prominent backing vocals. Morrison's rendition has not been officially released, unlike DeShannon's.

With manager Mary Martin (who renegotiated the Warner Bros. deal) having returned to New York, Morrison had been self-managing after moving to California. But after a period, he took on new help in the form of Stephen Pillster, who became general manager of Caledonia Productions: as announced in *Billboard* in October 1973. A local Bay-area manager, Pillster hired publicist Cynthia Copple, who produced a booklet of press clippings as *Reliable Sources*. Meanwhile, Morrison reputedly took a slot playing his favourite records on local San Rafael radio station KTIM.

Across 1973 and into 1974, Morrison performed live nearly 200 times, making these his most prolific concert years of the decade. Touring in 1973 began with a concert at The Lion's Share on 15 February, with Messenger, Labes, Schroer, Shlosser and bassist Marty David. There were early and late shows broadcast on Berkeley's KPFA radio station. Bootlegged as *The Lion Roars*, the two sets were not the same. Just two tracks featured from the then-latest album – 'Listen To The Lion' and 'Saint Dominic's Preview' – and two tracks from the forthcoming release: 'Wild Children' and 'Hard Nose The Highway'. There were outings for 'Misty' (arranged by Doug Messenger in Louis-Prima style), Fred Neil's 'Everybody's Talkin'', Hank Williams' 'Hey Good Lookin'', and, perhaps surprisingly, 'The White Cliffs Of Dover' referencing Little Jimmy in the lyric. Maybe the last choice – a song Van has only played in concert a few more times – is reflected in the *Hard Nose the Highway* album art. Rob Springett painted the gatefold cover after conversations with Morrison about his inspirations for the forthcoming album. It represents the two halves of the record well, with Van turning his back on the more seamy sides of street life, to face figures striding across the green fields and white cliffs beside a blue ocean above which bluebirds fly (perhaps suggesting that 'There There Child' was at one point intended for the album).

After inaugurating the year at The Lion's Share in February, there were appearances at theatres across California until the end of June – including an 18 April performance at the Shrine Auditorium in L.A., recorded for the TV show *Don Kirschner's Rock Concert*. The band were an early version of the Caledonia Soul Orchestra: James Trumbo: piano, Tim Kovatch: violin, Bill Atwood and Keith Johnson: trumpet, David Hayes: bass, John Platania: guitar, Dahaud Shaar: drums, and the ever-present Jack Schroer on sax. Footage shows Morrison dressed in a black Stetson hat and neckerchief, driving the band forward on rocking versions of 'I've Been Working', 'Caravan', 'Gloria' and 'Cyprus Avenue'. In the middle of the set came an early, slow and perhaps superior 'Flamingos Fly': more like the 1974 version on *The Philosopher's Stone*. In his *Astral Weeks* essay, Lester Bangs meditated on a clip of the song he saw on television that year:

> ...a late night network-TV rock concert: Van and his band come out, strike
> a few shimmering chords, and for about ten minutes, he lingers over

the words…, repeated slowly, again and again, distended, permutated, turned into scat, suspended in space and then scattered to the winds, muttered like a mantra till they turn into nonsense syllables, then back into the same soaring image as time seems to stop entirely. He stands there with eyes closed, singing, transported, while the band poises quivering over great open-tuned deep blue gulfs of their own.

Come mid-May, the definitive Caledonia Soul Orchestra had taken shape, and was in residence for a run of seven Troubadour gigs at the end of the month. It was decided to add strings to the regular six-piece line-up of Platania, Labes, Shaar, Hayes, Schroer, and Atwood. The string section – playing Jef Labes' arrangements – were Tom Halpin, Nate Rubin, and Tim Kovatch (violins), with Terry Adams (cello) and Nancy Ellis (viola): members of the Oakland Symphony Orchestra. When Morrison put a band together to play the *Astral Weeks* concerts in 2008, Adams and Ellis were recalled. They can be heard on the album recorded at the November Hollywood Bowl concerts.

By the start of July, the band were playing outside California: Milwaukee, Toronto, Montreal, Pittsburgh and New York. By month's end, they were performing in Europe: Amsterdam, Rotterdam, and Birmingham before the famous Rainbow concerts in London on 23/24 July. *It's Too Late to Stop Now* was partially recorded there, along with The Troubadour in May and the Santa Monica Civic in June.

In his interview with Bob Harris before the final Rainbow show, Morrison said they cut about 30 tracks for *Hard Nose the Highway*. Though some of the others were taped in early-1973, most were recorded at Caledonia Studio late in 1972. Yet, Warner Bros. only wanted a single album. Morrison told Harris he expected to look at writing some 'movie scores', which could've made for fascinating listening, especially as he'd also been working on a film script for 'Madame George' (presumably, this was also to include 'Madame Joy') with Joe O'Connell.

After London, Morrison played Bristol, Manchester, and Newcastle. He appeared on the cover of *Melody Maker*, where he was interviewed by Richard Williams, saying his next release would be a Christmas album, mentioning 'Chestnuts roasting': the image that appears in 'Autumn Song'. Warner Bros. announced two Dublin shows for the European tour, but they were never scheduled. August found the band again in California.

Morrison was however to appear in the Irish capital before the end of the year. At a concert recorded for TV at Dublin's RTE studio, he played

13 songs – five from the new album, plus 'Madame George', 'Beside You', 'Slim Slow Slider', 'And it Stoned Me', 'Saint Dominic's Preview', and three songs he planned to release in the 1970s but didn't: 'I Shall Sing', Hank Thompson's tribute to marriage breakdown and honky-tonk angels in 'The Wild Side Of Life', and the aforementioned Irish-set 'Drumshanbo Hustle' drawing on an incident at the town's Mayflower ballroom.

This last song was one of the few included in the actual broadcast, and Morrison said it would be on his next album, which he thought was already planned to come out sometime after the live set. Among the *Hard Nose the Highway* numbers, Morrison played 'Autumn Song' for what appears to be the only time live (as a request from his accompanying friend: Belfast journalist Donal Corvin). He also explained the crossed wires over playing Dublin, stating he would be back in March.

Van took the TV show opportunity to tour his home island in the autumn. This was a chance to develop more new material for the next album: most of which would be recorded at Caledonia Studio later that November. The result was to be another masterpiece, inspired by visions of Ireland and Morrison's transatlantic muse.

1974: It's Too Late to Stop Now and Veedon Fleece

It's Too Late to Stop Now (1974)

Personnel:
Van Morrison: vocals, arrangements
David Hayes: bass, backing vocals
Terry Adams: cello
Bill Atwood: trumpet, backing vocals
Nancy Ellis: viola
Tom Halpin, Tim Kovatch, Nathan Rubin: violin
Jef Labes: organ, piano, arrangements
John Platania: guitar, backing vocals
Jack Schroer: saxophone, tambourine, arrangements
Dahaud Shaar: drums, backing vocals
Producers: Van Morrison, Ted Templeman
All songs by Van Morrison except where stated
Recorded at The Troubadour, The Santa Monica Civic and The Rainbow – 24 May to 24 July 1973.
Release date: February 1974
Chart places: US: 53, UK: 167 (in 2008 – didn't chart in 1974)
Running time: 92:33
Tracklisting: Side One: 1. 'Ain't Nothin' You Can Do' (D. Malone, J. Scott), 2. 'Warm Love', 3. 'Into The Mystic', 4. 'These Dreams Of You', 5. 'I Believe To My Soul' (Ray Charles). Side Two: 1. 'I've Been Working', 7. 'Help Me' (Sonny Boy Williamson II, Willie Dixon, Ralph Bass), 8. 'Wild Children', 9. 'Domino', 10. I Just Want To Make Love To You' (Willie Dixon) .Side Three: 1. 'Bring it On Home To Me' (Sam Cooke), 2. 'Saint Dominic's Preview', 3. 'Take Your Hands Out Of My Pocket' (Sonny Boy Williamson II), 4. 'Listen To The Lion' .Side Four:1. 'Here Comes The Night' (Bert Berns), 2. 'Gloria', 3. 'Caravan', 4. 'Cyprus Avenue'.
Bonus track on the 2008 remaster: 'Brown Eyed Girl'

From the point of view of the fan, it's hard not to see 1974 as an early-career pinnacle for Morrison. Arguably, Van released two of the greatest records of the decade with *It's Too Late to Stop Now* and *Veedon Fleece*, bringing his total of solo LPs in the seven years after *Blowin' Your Mind!*, to eight, with at least another couple of albums of excellent material left unreleased. One of those recorded but mothballed songs – 'Feedback On Highway 101' – surfaced in February in a Johnny Winter cover version on his album *Saints and Sinners*. Much to the surprise of almost everyone,

Morrison also released a midyear swing single. Though spelt 'Caledonia' on that release, it was actually Louis Jordan's 1945 jump-blues 'Caldonia (What Makes Your Big Head So Hard?)', which Jordan had re-recorded with twanging guitar in 1956, and which James Brown laid down with added soul in 1964. Muddy Waters' performed it with The Band at *The Last Waltz*: available on that concert's deluxe edition.

On 27 May 1974, the BBC showed the 1973 Rainbow Theatre video as part of *The Old Grey Whistle Test* TV show. It was broadcast simultaneously on FM radio. This was one of the earliest stereo radio broadcasts, and the first simultaneous television/radio transmission of a rock concert (the 9-track recording of the show was released on DVD with the 2016 *It's Too Late to Stop Now Vol. II, III and IV* set). Meanwhile, Morrison was busy touring with the Caledonia Soul Express: a descendant of the Caledonia Soul Orchestra. In July, he played the first Knebworth festival with a lineup of Peter Van Hooke: drums, Pete Wingfield: piano, and Jerome Rimson: bass (They'd also been filmed ten days earlier for the German music show *Musikladen*). By the end of 1974, and still a young man in his 20s, Morrison was close to burnout from the slog of the last ten years and his battling with labels and the press.

But musically, the year had been a stellar one. The first fruits of Morrison's labour came in February with the quintessential double-live set *It's Too Late to Stop Now* – regularly acknowledged as one of the finest live albums ever made, despite relatively poor initial sales. No overdubs were added, which is why the recording of 'Moondance', which contained a bum guitar note, was not present. Named after the 'Caledonia Soul Music' outtake from a few years earlier, the 11-piece Caledonia Soul Orchestra provided a blend of band, strings and brass. ·

The May 2015 edition of *Uncut* carried the band members' stories of the shows. Jef Labes – who led the musicians, and whose mid-1973 departure for other projects possibly precipitated the end of the Caledonia Soul Orchestra – noted the overall approach:

> We majorly rearranged a lot of his old songs, like 'Cyprus Avenue', and [Morrison] also was revisiting a lot of old blues and R&B. Ray Charles, Sam Cooke, Sonny Boy Williamson: he was blowing that stuff brilliantly.

The album starts in a loud and brassy style with a song that Van used to cover with Them – Bobby Bland's 'Ain't Nothing You Can Do', highlighting how the Caledonia Soul Orchestra could play R&B as well as reinvent Morrison's old acoustic numbers. Bassist David Hayes knew the concerts were special at the time: 'The focus among all of us was sometimes so powerful, that when we topped that wave on something like 'Listen To The Lion', you could actually see it in the atmosphere! It was transcendental. I don't think I've ever gotten that with anybody else'. Hayes also commented on the relaxed interactions with Morrison, who showed great confidence in the players: 'He didn't micromanage the band, he left it to Jef and us. It wasn't very sophisticated; the stage setup was pretty simple. I don't even think we had monitors when we played The Troubadour, but we were a low-volume band with hardly any equipment, and we could hear each other pretty well'. At the peak of the tour – when Morrison's showmanship was at its height – Hayes noted that Van's use of suspense, silence, and sheer theatre, created astonishing tension and a sense of exhilaration: 'I really remember The Rainbow. The excitement around that was pretty extraordinary. The electricity was tangible. I found it quite startling what a big deal it was, him playing in London again. I think it was a big deal for him too. He was coming home in a sense, and I'm sure he was aware of it'.

While 'Ain't Nothing You Can Do' was chosen for the first single, Willie Dixon's classic 'I Just Want To Make Love To You' closes side one, following the request in the immediately preceding song 'Domino': to hear some rhythm and blues. The Dixon song has been recorded by over 100 artists, from Muddy Waters' original (under the title 'Just Make Love to Me') to B. B. King, Etta James, Chuck Berry, and The Rolling Stones. Paying his dues to those who inspired him, Van's live double album showcases other songs to acknowledge his musical roots – Sam Cooke's 'Bring It On Home To Me', Ray Charles' 'I Believe To My Soul' (straight after the mention of Charles in 'These Dreams Of You'), Sonny Boy Williamson's 'Take Your Hand Out Of My Pocket', and the 12-bar blues 'Help Me': first recorded by Williamson and based on Booker T. & the M.G.'s' 'Green Onions'. Alongside alternative live versions, there are more songs on the 3-CD release. *It's Too Late to Stop Now Volumes Vol. I, III and IV,* including the version of 'Moondance', left off the original live album. But of particular value – alongside a live version of 'There There Child' – are the songs not available elsewhere: 'No Way', 'I Paid The Price', 'Since I Fell For You', 'Bueno Sera' and 'Hey Good Lookin''.

After re-recording two of the *Veedon Fleece* tracks in New York in March ('Bulbs' and 'Cul De Sac'), a standalone single was recorded with the Caledonia Soul Express in the Netherlands in April, comprising

Morrison's take on the above-mentioned 'Caldonia' (which he likely knew from versions by Duke Ellington and Erskine Hawkins), and his own song, B-side 'What's Up Crazy Pup?'. With a lyric confined to the title refrain, the B-side most resembles a style Morrison was to return to, accompanied by Georgie Fame in the new century. As the lighthearted title suggests, it's feel-good concert jazz; the most striking thing being the utter contrast with anything else Morrison released that year – as if reminding everyone he's a musician who channels all kinds of genres, not just songs in the mystical vein he had reopened on the already-recorded *Veedon Fleece*. Accordingly, 'What's Up Crazy Pup?' was covered in 1982 by good-time ska band Bad Manners, after they'd included 'Caledonia' on their Two Tone Records debut a couple of years earlier.

1974 was to be another long year of touring, with gigs in every month, clocking up nearly 100. The only *Veedon Fleece* song given much concert time was the single 'Bulbs', though unreleased songs like 'Naked In The Jungle', 'Twilight Zone', and even 'Foggy Mountain Top', featured many times. Some *Veedon Fleece* songs – like 'Come Here My Love', 'Comfort You' and 'Linden Arden Stole The Highlights' – don't appear to have ever been performed live.

The touring year started in Texas in January, then headed to the West Coast, including a gig at the Winterland that produced rare video footage of – among many others – disparate classic tracks like 'Streets Of Arklow', the Dylan cover 'Just Like A Woman', 'Try For Sleep' and 'Wonderful Remark', before heading east and on to Europe. Though reinvented and slimmed down to the Caledonia Soul Express, for a while, Morrison still called the band the Caledonia Soul Orchestra when introducing them (usually during 'Caravan'), as at the Winterland: David Shaar: drums, James Trumbo: keyboards, David Hayes: bass, Ralph Wash: guitar, Jim Rothermel: sax. Others occasionally joined, such as brother-and-sister backing vocal team Dorothy Morrison and Bill Combes, at the Winterland, where Jack Schroer also appeared for his last Morrison gig. The Winterland performance of 'Listen To The Lion' is notable for demonstrating Van's long-standing custom of adding lines from other songs towards the end of a number. Here he sings most of the closing lines from the nearly-never-performed 'Autumn Song' from the last album. (These almost-spoken lines about beauty and peace are incidentally absent from the gatefold lyrics on *Hard Nose the Highway,* though they appear in the 'New Selected Lyrics' for Morrison's second volume of collected lyrics *Keep 'Er Lit*.) Also, while *Veedon Fleece* was unreleased,

Morrison added the chorus line 'You don't pull no punches, but you don't push the river' to the end of 'Caravan', and, most famously, he ends 'Cyprus Avenue' on the live album with the title-phrase 'It's Too Late To Stop Now': a line from 'Into The Mystic'.

Other concert recordings from the tour reveal interesting song choices. The FM broadcast of the early Cambridge, Mass show of 14 March includes all four of the longest *Astral Weeks* songs and has pre-release outings of 'What's Up Crazy Pup?' and 'Caldonia', with its 'What makes your big head so hard' foot stomp. While concerts in England failed to materialise in late March, Morrison played a string of gigs in Dublin while suffering from the flu: conscious of having disappointed people in Ireland in 1973. Next were performances in France, Germany, Belgium, Denmark, and the Netherlands, finishing in Britain with two nights at the Hammersmith Odeon. Van then headed back to the States in April to wind up the Caledonia Soul Express at the end of May, just as their one recording credit of 'Caledonia' was issued.

While it would be 1979 before Morrison played in Belfast, he returned to Europe for some further dates in June, following an appearance at the Montreux Jazz Festival on the last day of May. The concert was released in 2006 as the *Live at Montreux* DVD, coupled with a 1980 performance there. At the 1974 festival, Morrison played an experimental set (with the exception of 'Street Choir') featuring the as-then unreleased tracks, 'Twilight Zone', 'I Like It Like That' (from the Them days), 'Foggy Mountain Top', 'Bulbs', 'Swiss Cheese' (still unreleased), 'Heathrow Shuffle', 'Naked In The Jungle', a final instrumental harmonica boogie performance inspired by Hooker's 'Boogie Chillen'', and an encore of Lenny Welch's 'Since I Fell For You'. This encore was after a famous disagreement with a front-row audience member who didn't approve of the song choices, to which Morrison replied angrily that he would play what he liked. The hastily assembled band included bassist Jerome Rimson (who rejoined the touring band in the mid-1980s), drummer Dallas Taylor (who backed Crosby, Stills & Nash), and keyboardist (including the Wurlitzer organ) Pete Wingfield (whose high-pitched doo-wop pastiche 'Eighteen With A Bullet' was a 1975 top-20 hit on both sides of the Atlantic). The Montreux set signalled the beginning of another creative phase, as Morrison needed a fresh start after playing so many familiar songs night after night.

The band had recorded some tracks at Wisseloord Studios in Hilversum the week before. Though intended for *Veedon Fleece*, the recordings only surface on *The Philosopher's Stone* ('Foggy Mountain Top', 'Twilight Zone', 'Flamingos Fly'). A few more European concerts led up to the Knebworth festival appearance on 20 July. Future long-term band member Peter Van Hooke took over on drums after Montreux, joining Wingfield, Rimson and Morrison, whose saxophone and harmonica-playing could take more prominence in the small band.

It would be two years before Morrison played Europe again. The rest of 1974 saw North American concerts only. These started at The Orphanage in San Francisco, of which there's video footage from 29 July – the set filmed for the local PBS station to broadcast excerpts. The players at the next few gigs (the Great American Music Hall in San Francisco, and auditoriums in Minneapolis and Milwaukee) were an alternative group formed mainly from the band Sound Hole, who were Clover's main rivals in Marin County. The band now had brass to the fore: John Colla: alto sax, Brian Hogan: tenor sax, Bill Gibson: drums, Greg Douglass: guitar (after Dennis Langevin initially), John Farey: keyboards, and Mario Cipollina: bass. After a short break, Hooke, Rimson, and Wingfield returned in the autumn, heading east across the country and then back to California for a string of engagements, including the usual Canada stops, this time at Toronto's Maple Leaf Gardens.

Veedon Fleece (1974)

Personnel:

Van Morrison: guitar, vocals

David Hayes: bass

Jim Rothermel: flute, recorder

Nathan Rubin: violin

Theresa 'Terry' Adams: cello

Jack Schroer: soprano saxophone

Dahaud Shaar: drums

James Trumbo: piano

Ralph Wash: guitar

Jef Labes: piano ('Bulbs', 'Cul De Sac'), string and woodwind arrangements

Allan Schwarzberg: drums on ('Bulbs', 'Cul De Sac')

John Tropea: guitar ('Bulbs', 'Cul De Sac')

Joe Macho: bass ('Bulbs', 'Cul De Sac')

Producer: Van Morrison

All songs by Van Morrison

Recorded at Caledonia Studio (November 1973); Mercury Studios, New York,

March 1974
Release date: October 1974
Chart places: US: 53, Uk: 41
Running time: 47:36
Tracklisting: Side One: 1. 'Fair Play', 2. 'Linden Arden Stole The Highlights', 3. 'Who Was That Masked Man', 4. 'Streets Of Arklow', 5. 'You Don't Pull No Punches, But You Don't Push The River'. Side Two: 1. 'Bulbs', 2. 'Cul De Sac', 3. 'Comfort You', 4. 'Come Here My Love', 5. 'Country Fair'

During the band switchover came the release of *Veedon Fleece* in early October. As with so many 1970s Morrison albums, the story of its production focuses more on the previous year. The Ireland trip that began on 20 October 1973 was his first return to his homeland for half a dozen years. From a base in Dublin, he visited places mentioned in the *Veedon Fleece* songs (Killarney and Arklow), but also ones that are not (including Cork and Cashel).

These excursions into the Irish countryside fuelled numerous songs that would form the body of *Veedon Fleece,* and on Van's return to Fairfax the band went through a few of the new compositions each day. Jef Labes then added strings and flute, the album largely substituting the brass of previous records with woodwind.

The album's mood suggests a collection of associated pieces that come closer to being a song cycle than anything since *Astral Weeks*. The first word of the first song title is 'Fair' ('Fair Play), and the last word of the last song title is also 'Fair' ('Country Fair'). In terms of time, the opening song is about revisiting Ireland and taking in its verdant scenery. The final song is about the past – a time of innocence in the country – like the story recounted in 'And It Stoned Me'. The casual listener probably thinks Morrison is singing about a fair in 'Country Fair', but the word is again used as an adjective, the song having the same subject, with a different temporal setting, as the opening track – of taking in the surrounding beauty and pleasures of the countryside; watching the river flow, lying in the grass and feeling the cool summer night air without imagining times like these will ever cease.

At its heart, *Veedon Fleece* stands as a transatlantic view of Irish heritage from the perspective of a visiting exile. Side one rivals those first sides of *Astral Weeks* and *Moondance* in terms of bordering on perfection. Side one's five songs were all written during the three-week Ireland tour. The opener 'Fair Play' fuses Irish sayings and casual conversation with images, writers, and expressions from Ireland and the US. 'Fair play to you' was a phrase that travelling companion Donal Corvin used a great deal. The dreamlike beauty of the Killarney lakes becomes a jumping-off point for tales of mystery and imagination inspired by an Edgar Allan Poe paperback. The song begins a run of references to cowboy and Indian figures across first three songs – the Lone Ranger ('Hi-ho Silver') and Geronimo, the outlaw prototype Linden Arden, and then the return of the Lone Ranger as the third song's masked man. Three 19th-century writers are mentioned in 'Fair Play', suggesting Morrison was both reading them at the time, and taking inspiration from each. The first is Poe – an author of Irish heritage on his father's side, who, as an infant, was adopted by Scottish emigrants the Allans. The last is Thoreau – a transcendentalist writer to whom Morrison was temperamentally suited. He seemingly links the Killarney lakes to Thoreau's stories of experiencing nature and contemplating spirituality at Walden Pond in his famous reflective treatise on self-reliance, *Waldon*. Though no reason beyond Morrison's reading need be given for his inclusion, Oscar Wilde crops up in the middle– perhaps mentioned for being an Irishman who achieved fame for the first time when he toured America, in the early-1880s.

The song's instrumentation complements its return to nature, beginning with acoustic guitar, Trumbo's gentle piano, and Hayes' tripping bass. The lyric's key word is 'mind' and the song discusses the ways in which the scenery, Morrison's companion, and inspirational literature have enriched his interior life to produce the side-one song-suite that 'Fair Play' begins. The lyric talks about the mind appreciating architecture, providing determination to continue, and about a mind filled with fabulous stories and tales. This last point is precisely where the other side-one tracks merge – wild tales of mythical Irishman Linden Arden in San Francisco, of the Lone Ranger in the Wild West, of walking with a head full of poetry through the Garden of Ireland – the streets of the Viking settlement of Arklow – and finally the search for the Veedon Fleece itself.

In terms of the second and third tracks (which are a diptych of sorts), it's worth pointing out that the key to 'Linden Arden' is in the final line of 'Who Was That Masked Man' – 'There's good and evil in everyone' – given that the portrayal of Arden is full of stark contrasts in human behaviour, such as going to church and being a 'drinking man', having a love for children and using extreme violence. We can also note in passing that Linden Arden's story was turned into a play by Colin Mitchell: first performed at the 2014 Hollywood Fringe Festival.

'Streets Of Arklow' meditates on nature's ability to cleanse the soul through a long immersion in the landscape and having the determination, 'the mind', to press on to dawn. This seems in part to be about experiencing Ireland and the countryside both as God's green land of beauty in the spirit of a tale of mystery and imagination. Linking back to the 'meadow's way' of 'Fair Play', the name Arklow is derived from the Old Norse words 'meadow of Arnkell', and the town is situated in the County of Wicklow, whose Old Norse name Víkingaló means Vikings' Meadow. Jim Rothermel s recorder is the song's dominant instrument, and his flute and recorder-playing is the album's most arresting musical feature, bringing a unique quality to the closing song 'Country Fair'.

Side one's last track is the epic 'You Don't Pull No Punches, But You Don't Push the River', from which the album title is drawn (still the longest track on the album, 'You Don't Pull No Punches, But You Don't Push The River' was cut down from its full 12 minutes). The concept of the Veedon Fleece has no external reference, but returning to the emphasis on mind, Morrison associated its quest with Gestalt therapy, and the 'fleece' may be a simple reference to Jason, or to Viking heritage and the importance of wool for the Norsemen's sails and clothes. The song title draws on Barry Stevens' autobiographical journal *Don't Push The River (It flows by itself)* (1970). The book recounts a three-month period at the Gestalt Institute of Canada in 1969; Stevens' investigations of Gestalt Therapy, Zen Buddhism, Native American religious practices and the Indian philosopher adopted by the Theosophists, J. Krishnamurti. The word Gestalt has no English translation but denotes how the individual doesn't perceive in bits and pieces but in patterned wholes. This could be considered as one way to read the album and Morrison's westward journey along the river/stream of consciousness, taking in William Blake's *The Book of Urizen* and the Sisters of Mercy. But the references most likely reflect Morrison's reading at the time, and his search for soul satisfaction – therefore, he also talks of contemplating Meher Baba, whose writings on spiritual consciousness were a syncretic blend of Sufi, Vedic, and Yogic teachings. In terms of the quest motif that drives the song, the name Veedon Fleece can be taken as a combination of Eastern and Western mythology; of the ancient Hindu Vedas and the golden fleece beyond the edge of the known world. Yet, the album title remains distinctly enigmatic. Morrison once said it was an invented name, therefore akin to Linden Arden, and Veedon Fleece was one of a number of characters he wanted to put into song – which is probably the best way to think of many of his literary references: not so much as authors, but characters. In terms of the song's musical legacy, if Veedon Fleece were indeed a character, then it's possible she resurfaces as the protagonist in one of the most beautiful homages to Morrison's music: a track called 'Home Life' on Shearwater's 2008 album *Rook.* It starts with a similar guitar phrase and an opening piano melody that's identical to Morrison's epic song before beginning with the exact same first line about a tomboy.

Though less famous than other recordings, these five tracks constitute a remarkable run of excellent material. As noted, this makes side one of *Veedon Fleece* a contender for the best side of vinyl in Morrison's extraordinary catalogue. Labes' string and wind arrangements are first class, gelling the players into a unified soundscape; utilizing the core of the Caledonia Soul Orchestra; Ralph Wash's acoustic guitar swapped in for Platania's electric. Jim Stern, Dahaud, and Jean Shaar engineering the set, along with Elvin Campbell, who presumably took the controls in New York.

The New York recordings introduce a noticeable shift in pace at the start of side two. With the opening brace of tracks having been re-recorded in NY to create a single, they diverge from the feel and rhythm of the rest of the album, which is why the A-side 'Bulbs' (with John Tropea's country guitar) and its US B-side 'Cul De Sac' stand out from the rest of the record. Tropea remembers: 'We did 'Bulbs' and 'Cul De Sac' at Mercury Studios in New York. It was a double date, from 10 until 5. Van would run down the music, we'd do one or two takes, then I stayed to do the solo on 'Bulbs''. 'Bulbs' was the album's only single (coupled with 'Who Was That Masked Man' in the UK).

'Bulbs' is a fine up-tempo track, even though it jars a little with the album's other songs – its lyric seemingly about the effects of the music business lifestyle – or showbiz – that burns out all the young hopefuls who try to make it in America. 'Cul De Sac' is about distances travelled, inside and out. In its universal message of authenticity, it references the Mount Palomar observatory: it's who you are that counts, not who you know. One of the alternative versions of 'Cul De Sac', a mellower, shorter, and arguably better version, more in keeping with the rest of the album, was already in the can as far back as the *Hard Nose the Highway* sessions. This is probably the version issued as a bonus on the 2008 remaster of *Veedon Fleece*, along with a shorter six-minute version of the falsetto track 'Twilight Zone' that appeared on *The Philosopher's Stone*.

The final three songs – 'Comfort You', 'Come Here My Love' and 'Country Fair' – return to side one's simple acoustic feel, with lyrics focusing on love and communion. In fact, they blend very well into a short meditative song sequence. 'Comfort You' is almost a mantra focused on shouldering the burden of loved ones. 'Come Here My Love' is one of Morrison's most beautiful love songs, with an enigmatic lyric, seemingly composed after returning from Ireland. It leads into 'Country Fair' by speaking of becoming enraptured and intrigued by beauty and especially by all that can be seen and heard in nature. It also returns us to the themes of 'Fair Play' and the banality of words besides the contemplation of trees and meadows. 'Country Fair' meditatively underlines the musical stillness and peace that have characterised much of the album while repeating its message of harmony found in nature and contemplative beauty.

David Hayes notes of much of the album's material that Morrison 'hasn't ever played those songs live. They were really hard to perform after the fact because they're basically unrepeatable. It took so much focus and concentration to make those things lift up, it's very difficult to recreate them. So *Veedon Fleece* really captures a moment in time'.

And so it seemed, as the album met with a mooted response in late 1974, its exceptional quality only apparent to a majority of critics in subsequent years. But this did not help his confidence levels at the time, and Van appeared unsure of his next direction: his batteries corroded like one of the characters in 'Bulbs'. Plus, the entire effort around the album's production and marketing was arguably too restrained and undemonstrative. The artwork was suitably green, but its sombre colours were unlikely to catch the eye of record buyers, with Tom Collins' solemn cover photograph of a besuited Morrison, shot in 1973 at the Sutton House Hotel near Donal Corvin's home in the Dublin suburbs. The two Irish wolfhounds just happened to be there, and the cover is no more evocative or representative of Morrison's normal life than the *Tupelo Honey* cover.

The year's last gig was at the Keystone in Berkeley on 30 December – a tribute concert for friend Tex Coleman who needed to pay medical expenses. Morrison played blues with the Elvin Bishop band: 'Trouble in Mind', 'Help Me', 'Bring It On Home to Me', 'Swing It To Me' and 'Baby, Please Don't Go'. There had been no time for rehearsal, but it was a good opportunity for Morrison to let loose on sax and harmonica, with the set improvised as a blues jam, he and Bishop sharing vocals. Friend John Lee Hooker played the opening set, and this kind of evening probably fed into Morrison's thinking over the next two years – time to get back to his musical roots, collaborate with different people and find a new direction.

1975: Mechanical Bliss

For a *Stage Life* magazine interview, Morrison explained to Ritchie Yorke: 'I didn't seem to have anything to say in that period of time after the '74 tour. There was nothing definite that I wanted to record. Some thoughts went through my head about recording some stuff that had influenced me earlier in my career, like blues and early rock. But it didn't seem to really make sense at that point – it might've been taken the wrong way'. He said this in 1977, after he'd had ample opportunity to digest the events of the last two years, during which time he had material to release and albums in mind but didn't bring any particular recording project to fruition; instead investigating different styles, often going back to his roots.

In 1975, Morrison continued working at Caledonia Studio but also increasingly made use of the Record Plant in Sausalito (where he was to record a lot of material in the early-1980s after cutting *Into the Music* there in 1979). He also continued to tour, playing a few dozen concerts, though all but one took place in California. The most common songs he performed were 'Wild Night' and 'Gloria', followed by 'Saint Dominic's Preview', into which, on half a dozen occasions, he introduced snatches of Lou Reed's 'Walk On The Wild Side' and a song he said he'd recently heard on the radio: The Rolling Stones' 'You Can't Always Get What You Want'. A rare acknowledgement of the work of his rock contemporaries, this, more importantly, suggested he was experimenting while deciding on his way forward.

Van's road band for most of 1975 comprised familiar players David Hayes and Mark Jordan, drummer Tony Dey from the Ted Ashford group, and guitarist John Blakely from California rock band Stoneground. These musicians played on a number of the Caledonia tracks that surfaced on *The Philosopher's Stone* – all four players appearing together on 'I Have Finally Come To Realise', 'Joyous Sound' and 'The Street Only Knew Your Name'. In concert, the band tried out standards like Rufus Thomas' 'Walking The Dog', Lead Belly's 'Sweet Mary Blues', and Mose Allison's 'One Of These Days': which Morrison included as the lead song on the 1996 collaboration album *Tell Me Something: The Songs of Mose Allison*.

In his 1974 interviews, Morrison had already trailed plans for a new album to follow *Veedon Fleece*. At Knebworth, for example, he'd declared the recordings were in the bag and the album was to be called 'Naked In The Jungle/Mechanical Bliss'. This has indeed become known as the 'lost' *Mechanical Bliss* album because a record with *that* title came the closest to realisation. However, alternative titles were suggested at the time, including *Not Working for You* and *Stiff Upper Lip*, and it's quite possible that other projects with different songs could've appeared. When subsequently prepared for a planned release, *Mechanical Bliss* was proposed as a nine-track album featuring most or all of the following songs – the uniquely idiosyncratic title track; the party-line freak-out '(This Is Not The) Twilight Zone'; the ya-na-ha jazz funk of 'Naked In The Jungle' (which had 1974 and 1975 versions); Van's take on the Jackie De Shannon tryout 'Flamingos Fly' (which he was to re-record in 1977); a tribute to influences such as Jimmie Rodgers' blue yodelling in 'Foggy Mountain Top (T for Texas)'; an early rendition of a soon-to-be-familiar song he'd considered recording as a duet with Bill Wyman: 'Joyous Sound'; a longer version of 'The Street Only Knew Your Name' (which was to be re-recorded for *Inarticulate Speech of the Heart*); the wake-up call that is 'I Have Finally Come To Realise', and finally the declarative ode to soulful spontaneity: 'When I Deliver'.

All but two of these songs turned up on *The Philosopher's Stone,* while 'Mechanical Bliss', became the B-side to the 1977 single 'Joyous Sound'. The first five recordings listed above had been set down in Hilversum in July 1974 with Rimson, Van Hooke and Wingfield, and the next three – which had all been recorded twice – were cut in California with the 1975 touring quartet, as was the still-unreleased blues 'When I Deliver'. This last recording was in fact slated for inclusion on the initial 1996 attempt to assemble *The Philosopher's Stone.* But by the time of its 1998 release, the song – along with the 1979 recordings 'John Brown's Body' and 'I'm Ready' – had been replaced.

The definitive 1975 *Mechanical Bliss* track list – if such a thing existed – might've differed slightly from the nine songs outlined above. By this time, other recordings were filling studio shelves, including an excellent piano version of a song called 'Street Theory': about returning to his boyhood stomping ground, sounding like a faster cousin of 'Come Running' (and sometimes called 'Come On Out Child'). It was recorded at the *Veedon Fleece* sessions in late 1973 and re-recorded at the same time as 'Caldonia' in April 1974. A later 1980 version appears on *The Philosopher's Stone*, with slightly modified lyrics, a different rhythm and prominent brass, making the song feel closer to *Beautiful Vision's* 'Cleaning Windows'. Several of the unreleased songs from around the *Hard Nose the Highway* sessions have already been discussed, but other unmentioned ones recorded in 1974 that could've appeared on a new 1975 album, are the instrumental 'Much Binding In The Marsh' (sometimes the last word is cited as March), which took its title from a radio comedy show about a fictional RAF station, 'Heathrow Shuffle', which was played at Montreux in 1974 and later featured on the live 1996 album *How Long Has This Been Going On,* and the saxophone instrumental 'Boffy Flow', which (with Spike Milligan's first name added) was transformed for *A Sense of Wonder* and *A Chieftains Celebration.*

More unreleased studio recordings followed in 1975: Merle Travis' coalminer lament about the truck system, 'Sixteen Tons', the too-much-pressure song '(I'm) Not Working For You', 'You Move Me' (a homage to Sonny Boy Williamson's blues standard 'Sugar Mama' – the flipside to 'Good Morning, School Girl'), a version of Little Willie John's 'All Around The World', a take on King Curtis' 'Reminiscing', a spirited wail through Ray Charles' 'Don't Change On Me', another wake-up-and-realise song 'Down To Earth', Arthur Alexander's 'It Hurts To Want It So Bad', and a medley of Johnny Kidd & the Pirates: 'I Go Ape/Shakin' All Over'. According to Clinton Heylin's sessionography, there were also recordings from the two years following *Hard Nose the Highway*, under the titles 'Sit There', 'Cool For Kats' and 'Talking Harp' (a term for playing the harp/harmonica in imitation of the voice: as associated with Sonny Terry).

Two further 1975 tracks appeared on *The Philosopher's Stone* – the traditional blues about steel-driver 'John Henry', and Lead Belly's cowboy song 'Western Plain'. As can be gathered by now, Morrison could well have released an album of blues covers or a tribute to the artists and songs that inspired him – just like David Bowie did two years earlier with *Pin Ups*, which included 'Here Comes The Night'. A couple of years later, as we'll see, Van hired that album's famed guitarist Mick Ronson for his onstage backing band, performing songs like 'Shakin' All Over'.

Many Morrison songs written around this time share certain themes – his childhood neighbourhood, the search for self-knowledge and enlightenment, and working for the (record) company man. He'd also begun writing the similarly themed 'Tore Down à La Rimbaud' positioning himself as a young burnt-out *poète maudit* (a poet dogged by misfortune and lack of recognition), wishing his muse would descend. (The song was reworked for 1985's *A Sense of Wonder.*)

Another 'theme' was Van's love of radio comedy. In 'Mechanical Bliss', for example, Morrison adopts a clipped upper-class English accent, name-dropping characters called Ponsonby-Smith and Caruthers, and introducing some wordless Milligan-esque vocal sounds. It ends with the invocation, 'Okay, chaps, stiff upper lip!'. In 2020, Morrison told Martin Chilton for the *Independent*:

> Oh, yeah. I remember 'Mechanical Bliss' well, because I also played piano on that... it's probably one of the only tracks where I played that many chords on piano. It was in A-flat, as far as I remember. It was just a take-off of British comedy – The Goons and such – which I had grown up enjoying. 'Stiff upper lip' and all that, right?

The *Mechanical Bliss* project progressed as far as the artwork for a possible release in early 1975, but was shelved for unknown reasons. Remarkably, the discarded cover image of monster-headed skyscrapers (combining a Zox painting with a Charlie Ganse photograph) was used almost unchanged (except for the addition of a man lying on a park bench) for Steely Dan's 1976 album *The Royal Scam*.

Taken as a whole, the range of material now available but unreleased in 1975, indicates not that Morrison lacked creative drive and energy, but that he was set on finding a new road and experimenting with styles. The tracks point to several possible directions: such as instrumental tracks, humorous songs, or a return to the blues. But the strings and acoustic instruments of *Veedon Fleece* have gone, and he clearly wished to do something different, as evident from his choice of musicians. The search for the next step took many months, during which Morrison was still busy. Recordings and shows continued, if not at pace. Finding a path was going to get harder before it got easier.

Van told the press that the spring 1975 concerts were also to be something new – featuring instrumentals, new songs drawing on his love of rock and roll, and R&B covers. New songs appearing in the set from April included 'Shake, Rattle And Roll', 'Walking The Dog' and 'Whole Lotta Shakin' Goin' On'. The opening number was the jazz standard 'Alright, Okay, You Win' (best known from Peggy Lee's 1958 recording), complementing the show closer of 'Moondance' segueing into Little Willie John's 'Fever' (also covered successfully by Lee in 1958). But in many ways, Morrison wasn't feeling it anymore, and the performances started to fizzle out after June. There were sporadic gigs but nothing amounting to a tour. Neither concert hall nor recording studio seemed to appeal much, though work went on. It was time for change and contemplation – a period of transition definitely – but to *what*, was unclear. Morrison was exploring philosophy and spirituality in his reading, coming to terms with hard drinking, studying voraciously – from existentialism to pastoral poetry – and revisiting instruments such as the saxophone, which he'd largely set aside to concentrate on singing.

In 1977, Morrison told *Rolling Stone*'s Cameron Crowe: 'I didn't really go anywhere. I just had to stop. I wasn't getting out of it what I wanted … it just wasn't worth the hotels and the airports and all that. I've been doing this since I was 12. I personally reached a place where I wanted to take it apart so I could put it together in a way that I could live with it and could maybe even be happy with it'. He explained that he nearly completed an LP with jazz producer Stewart Levine, accompanied by a one-off group including blues guitarist Arthur Adams and keyboardist Joe Sample from jazz-fusion group The Crusaders, but he 'backed off from it because it wasn't feeling right. I wasn't sure whether I wanted to do a whole album'. Producer Levine kept the tapes recorded at the Record Plant in October 1975. After his death, his son Sunny spoke of his father's recollection of the sessions:

> Morrison and the band got along great, and the sessions were a joyful experience. Morrison was very relaxed, and sounds extra soulful, as you can hear on the tape. The whole tracking experience was a pleasure, with no drama in sight. They went away for a week and planned to put the finishing touches on the record: which would have been the Tower of Power horns, followed by mixing. When they returned to the studio, Morrison and Levine had an argument that abruptly ended the sessions and that was that! The record was never released.

This did, however, leave nine unreleased recordings – 'You Move Me', 'Grits Ain't Groceries', 'Don't Change On Me', 'We're Gonna Make It', 'It Hurts To Want It So Bad', 'The Street Only Knew Your Name', 'Down To Earth', 'I Have Finally Come To Realise' and 'Joyous Sound'. 'Grits Ain't Groceries' was simply another name for the abovementioned 'All Around The World'. ('Grits Ain't Groceries' was the title used for Little Milton's 1969 hit version of the song, with 'All Around The World' as the sub-title). 'We're Gonna Make It' was another R&B classic (1965) by Little Milton, who later covered 'Tupelo Honey' for *Vanthology: A Tribute to Van Morrison* (2003).

Two curious points to note here – first, apropos Sunny Levine's story above, Morrison chants the title of Oakland soul/funk band Tower of Power's debut album *East Bay Grease* (1970) at the close of 'Gloria' on

It's Too Late to Stop Now. Secondly, Elvin Bishop Band singer Mickey Thomas picked up 'The Street Only Knew Your Name' for his debut solo album *As Long As You Love Me* (1977).

Still searching for direction at the end of 1975, Morrison decided to move on from the records he'd made since 1968. What he was searching for could be called the 'Veedon Fleece' or 'the lion'. It could be called transcendence, or it could be called something else that supersedes normal language. According to critic Greil Marcus, Morrison searches in this way for freedom. Marcus relayed critic Ralph J. Gleason saying that *Moondance* reminded him of a film biography he saw about Irish tenor John McCormack (whose voice Van's father loved). The film told of how McCormack told his accompanist that what separates an important voice from a good one is to have the 'yarragh' in it. For Marcus, this is part of the quest, and when Morrison's music comes together, 'the result can be a sort of mystical deliverance. The listener is not spared a single fear, but he or she is somehow insulated from all fears: as is the performer'.

Morrison clearly had the yarragh on 'When I Deliver': 1975's final studio recording (17 December: the last Record Plant session for a few years). On this, he sings his heart out and makes plain to the listener his musical quest. The lyric suggests his wait for the blues to come through in the moment. It's like searching for the philosopher's stone, but when it comes through on the tape machine, we can only call it a kind of mechanical bliss.

1976: The Last Waltz

1975 had been a low-profile year, with Morrison playing only two dozen gigs. In 1976 he would perform only as a guest on a few occasions and had only a handful of rehearsals and studio appearances.

His first foray into the studio was in March to record his own take on Ray Charles' 'What Would I Do' – another version was recorded for A Sense of Wonder in 1985. In the early 1960s, Morrison had played Germany with The Monarchs, singing Ray Charles songs to the homesick American G.I.s. The song was recorded at Los Angeles' Shangri-La studios: where Morrison had that month appeared with members of The Band on a studio jam for Eric Clapton's birthday. Van sang 'Who Do You Love', 'Stormy Monday', and 'Hard Times'. This preceded three guest appearances on Clapton's UK tour in August (Manchester, Birmingham, and London), singing 'Help Me', 'Kansas City', and 'Into The Mystic'.

Two weeks later, Morrison was at Richard Branson's The Manor studio with Ray Parker Jr., Dr. John, English jazz musician Chris Barber's band, and a number of players brought in for auditions. The one-track cut was the turn-of-the-century New Orleans funeral jazz classic 'Didn't He Ramble': derived from the English tall-tale folk song 'The Derby Ram'. We'll talk more about Dr. John in the next chapter, but both he and Barber collaborated with Morrison again later in their careers – notably at the gig that appeared as *The Skiffle Sessions – Live in Belfast 1998*: recorded with Lonnie Donegan at Whitla Hall (where in 1979 Morrison played his first Northern Ireland gigs of the decade). An important figure championing artists integral to Morrison's teenage years, Barber was a catalyst in the expanding music landscape of the 1950s and 1960s, bringing to the UK for the first time artists like Muddy Waters, Big Bill Broonzy, and Sonny Terry and Brownie McGhee. Barber had a crucial influence on the up-and-coming blues scene that founded the careers of the likes of Eric Clapton, Peter Green and The Rolling Stones.

As for 'Didn't He Ramble', Morrison would've known the song from the Barber band's 1955 recording on the National Jazz Federation album *Traditional Jazz at the Royal Albert Hall* (recorded in October 1954). Being a member of Chris Barber's Jazz Band at the time of the recording, Lonnie Donegan and his skiffle group also appear on the album. Morrison sang on the 1976 recording, but it actually appeared on a 2011 Barber anthology album called *Memories of My Trip*. (Barber owned a copy of the backing track minus the vocal until Morrison sent him his original vocal track: recombining the two.) The song appears heavily reworked (and credited to Morrison) as a bonus on the 2019 deluxe edition of his 1997 album *The Healing Game* – showing its influence on many of his lyrics, but particularly on another song expressing his search along the roads and highways: 'The Philosopher's Stone' (from *Back on Top* (1999)).

Still searching for the right direction, Morrison explained his dilemma to Ritchie Yorke for *Stage Life* in 1977:

> It wasn't exciting anymore to totally be a singer/songwriter because it wasn't working for me .... I had gotten to a point where I was definitely sure that I was on the wrong track after about 16 years. What excited me when I first came into it, was the performing aspect and doing blues-oriented material, rock/blues-oriented stuff, basic stuff; basic what they call rock 'n' roll. Then it evolved into more of a ballad-style singer/songwriter thing. And there was a conflict in trying to merge the two styles with the same band behind me, 'cause the musicians that I would need to do ballad-oriented tunes would require musicians who were more into jazz. But they couldn't cut rock. I had to be more limited and specific about what I was doing. So I realised that what I was looking for was doing collaborations with other people – people who can play a ballad, rock, jazz.

Morrison also guested on Rolling Stone Bill Wyman's *Stone Alone* album (1976), playing harmonica, guitar and alto saxophone on three tracks, including the single taken from the LP: a cover of the 1961 Gary U.S. Bonds hit 'Quarter To Three'. There was talk of doing a skiffle album together, though nothing came of it. But Wyman did put Morrison in touch with Harvey Goldsmith as someone who might help with business matters or even management. Arrangements were also made for Morrison to move back to the UK around this time, but at this point in his career, almost everything was more an exploration than a definite plan.

Because of the constant speculation about his whereabouts and intentions, he released not an album but a press statement in 1976: 'I've been trying out various experimental projects at various times and places. It's likely that a wide cross-section of these sessions will be released at a later date on a 'history of' sort of album'. He wanted a new perspective, to get back to his roots, back to basic rock 'n' roll, and even back home.

Van began hanging out in Los Angeles, renting a place in the West L.A. suburb of Brentwood. He was still looking for the best way to divest himself of the singer-songwriter mantle, and continued to revisit blues touchstones to reconnect with what got him into music in the first place. In a 1977 *NME* interview, he used the term 'identity crisis' in relation to his direction of exploration, asserting the need to find a unique path rather than conform to expectations – not least because he wished to still be digging the music at 40, rather than cashing in on whatever styles were in vogue. Ever the independent thinker, he was clearly considering the long term at a point when others were wondering whether he'd quit the business. Neil Young might again provide a comparison, as being someone who famously said that his 1972 success with *Harvest* 'put me in the middle of the road. Travelling there soon became a bore, so I headed for the ditch – a rougher ride, but I saw more interesting people there'. Young then produced what became known as his 'ditch trilogy' – *Time Fades Away, Tonight's the Night* and *On the Beach* – the latter (the last recorded if not released) being among his very finest. Morrison similarly took three albums to work through his dark night of the soul. But he was indeed meeting 'interesting people' along the way. (Other collaborations not yet mentioned, were mooted – with Al Kooper, Phil May from The Pretty Things, and Roger Chapman's band Streetwalkers, whose Bobby Tench would join Morrison in 1978). Young was also battling his demons while in the ditch – shelving recordings, including the excellent *Homegrown*, and occasionally re-recording material left in the can.

Young and Morrison appeared on the same bill in 1976 at The Band's Thanksgiving day farewell concert *The Last Waltz* (released as a movie in 1978). As Morrison leaves the stage high-kicking to 'Caravan', Robbie Robertson calls to the crowd, 'Van the Man!', creating a second nickname for Morrison after coining the alias 'the Belfast Cowboy' years earlier. Recalling their pairing on '4% Pantomime', Morrison's segment at *The Last Waltz* opened with a gritty and intense duet with The Band's pianist Richard Manuel – 'Tura Lura Lura': a version of James Royce Shannon's 'Too-Ra-Loo-Ra-Loo-Ral (That's An Irish Lullaby)'. Robertson and Morrison had discussed the performance at The Band's Shangri-La studio in Malibu, and they rehearsed it the day before the show.

With only six weeks to go before the planned date, Robertson called Martin Scorsese to ask if he'd direct *The Last Waltz* as a concert documentary. Scorsese was fully occupied making the musical drama *New York, New York* (his follow-up to *Taxi Driver*), but when Robertson mentioned some of the performers they'd lined up, the director jumped onboard – '*Van Morrison?* Are you *kidding? I have* to do it', he said:

reinforcing the intriguing rumour that Scorsese had based the first 15 minutes of *Taxi Driver* on 'Madame George'. In the end, he directed the concert recording using seven 35mm cameras.

As with Dylan, there seemed to be some concern that Morrison might be a no-show on the night: at least on the stage. At the rehearsal, he wore a private-detective raincoat, and Robertson urged him to do the same for the concert. But something evidently didn't sit well with Morrison. According to his new manager Harvey Goldsmith, after watching the first half of the gig, Morrison went back to the Miyako Hotel to change clothes. On returning, he was ready to go on stage in a maroon jumpsuit spangled with sequins, which was a brave and ultimately inspired decision. Greil Marcus' contemporary *Rolling Stone* concert review put it like this:

> Manuel turned the piano over to John Simon, and began 'Tura Lura' – a song about an Irish lullaby. Just as Manuel finished the first verse, Van Morrison made his entrance, and he turned the show 'round. I had seen him not many minutes before, prowling the balconies, dressed nondescriptly in a shirt and jeans, scowling. But there he was on stage in an absurd maroon suit and a green top, singing to the rafters. They cut into 'Caravan' – with John Simon waving The Band's volume up and down, and the horns at their most effective – while Van burned holes in the floor. He was magic, and I thought, 'Why didn't he join The Band years ago?'. More than any other singer, he fit in; his music and theirs made sense together. It was a triumph, and as the song ended, Van began to kick his leg in sheer exuberance, and he kicked his way right off stage like a Rockette. The crowd had given him a fine welcome, and they cheered wildly when he left.

Of course, Morrison had been doing this performance of 'Caravan' with high kicks and theatrics for years. It was the kind of overfamiliar crowd-pleasing he'd grown tired of, but for *The Last Waltz*, it was a triumph all the same. The Band drummer Levon Helm agreed in his book *This Wheel's On Fire*:

> By now, it was after midnight and the crowd was subdued. The momentum of the show had been lost halfway through Joni's set … this was Van's first appearance on stage in more than two years, and The Last Waltz was suddenly revived with a spectacular version of 'Caravan'. Van burned through his great song – 'Turn it up! Little bit louder! Radio!'

– complete with kick-steps across the stage at the end. Van turned the whole thing around. God bless him for being the showman he is.

Morrison returned to the stage at the end with most of the guest artists, sharing the main microphone with Dylan and Robertson for the choruses of 'I Shall Be Released': the song that had inspired 'Brand New Day' on *Moondance*. Talking to Cameron Crowe in 1977, Morrison noted:

> I never played with Bob before. It was a real highlight for me. I don't usually come out in situations like that. I didn't want the promotions ... but it was the right situation because of something karmic. One of the basic principles is that it was not hype. Robbie didn't want to hype it, and it wasn't hyped, it was a pure situation! That show couldn't be done – it's something that happens.

The comment reinforces his view that great performances have to be found and felt: channelled rather than put on. Something pure happened at *The Last Waltz*, even if it didn't tempt Morrison back into performing any time soon after. The experience nonetheless rekindled a fire in the belly, acting as a catalyst for his next project. In the interim, he continued looking for inspiration, in mythology, poetry, history, mystical writing, and classical music.

Meanwhile, Warner Bros. were getting twitchy about not having a record to release. Material from various sessions over the years was reviewed for a possible new album, pulling together bits and pieces, possibly to be called *Highlights*. A 14-track compilation was even assembled but was never issued. Morrison was still in the mood for collaborations and exploring his blues roots. This resulted in the 1977 release of his most unusual 1970s album, as he collaborated with someone who'd been at *The Last Waltz* and also at The Manor. But 1977 would not see Morrison return to live performance, and, once again, the recording of that forthcoming album started the year before.

1977: A Period of Transition

A Period of Transition (1977)

Personnel:

Van Morrison: guitar, harmonica, vocals

Mac Rebennack (Dr. John): keyboards; guitar ('It Fills You Up')

Ollie E. Brown: drums, percussion

Reggie McBride: bass

Marlo Henderson: guitar

Jerry Jumonville: tenor and alto Saxophone

Joel Peskin: baritone saxophone

Mark Underwood: trumpet

Carlena Williams, Gregory Wright, Toni McVey, Robbie Montgomery, Gerald Garrett, Roger Kennerly-Saint, Candy Nash, Paulette Parker, Joseph Powell: backing vocals

Producers: Van Morrison, Dr. John

All songs by Van Morrison

Recorded at The Manor, Oxfordshire late-1976

Release date: April 1977

Chart places: US: 43 US: 23

Running time: 34:12

Tracklisting: Side One: 1. 'You Gotta Make It Through The World', 2. 'It Fills You Up', 3. 'The Eternal Kansas City'. Side Two: 1. 'Joyous Sound', 2. 'Flamingos Fly', 3. 'Heavy Connection', 4. 'Cold Wind In August'

In the song 'Russian Roulette' on *Days Like This* (1995), Morrison sings about going down to New Orleans to see Dr. John, to find some peace from bad thoughts, and stop pointing the proverbial gun at his own head. Dr. John – Louisiana musician Mac Rebennack – seems to have had a reassuring influence. When the two met via *The Last Waltz,* Morrison said he wanted to do a tribute record to the R&B that had inspired him. So, later in 1976, they recorded together, with Dr. John as musician, producer, and arranger. Asked to employ a rhythm section, he picked up players from Stevie Wonder's Wonderlove band – drummer Ollie Brown and bassist Reggie McBride on bass, plus Ray Parker, Jr. on rhythm guitar. Parker was soon let go, so Dr. John and Morrison ended up splitting the guitar parts between them, with Marlo Henderson – also from Wonderlove – brought in to overdub lead guitar in L.A. Dr. John later remembered it all as confusion:

The same troubles hampered our work throughout these sessions. I had written some horn charts for the album and came to the studio ready to do the horns, but Van had fired most of the horn section! We had to wing it with just Jerry Jumonville and Joel Peskin on saxes: a sudden change of direction that made the horn charts useless because I had written them for six horns.

In his *Rolling Stone* review of the album, Greil Marcus blamed the horns for the record's dull sound. For Morrison, *A Period of Transition* was the means to move forward – a record that marked the time when he was digesting new influences and looking back to the music that had shaped him.

A Period of Transition has a consistency: for one thing, it comprises a new set of original compositions all recorded with the same musicians. There are some excellent songs too, if few transcendent moments, but the sound is indeed quite dull. The engineer was Gary Ladinsky, but assistant Mick Glossop went on to engineer Morrison's next two albums. With seven songs, the album has the same number of tracks as *Saint Dominic's Preview,* but it has neither that album's expansive settings nor the power of its set-pieces, like 'Listen To The Lion', 'Almost Independence Day' or 'Saint Dominic's Preview'.

The album title is reflected in the cover photos, which show Morrison moving through a series of expressions indicating different moods, with appropriate lighting and framing. The back cover assigns the concept to him, and features a full-size black and white photograph of Van – the colour version of which appears as the first shot on the front: beside the title but torn off at the bottom. Photographer Ken McGowan's 15 snapshots of Morrison are suggestive of the singer's phases since 1974, and the record's musical genres.

The songs are indeed varied. There's the pure pop elation of 'Joyous Sound', the swinging jazz optimism of taking a trip to where 'Flamingos Fly', a classic ballad in 'Heavy Connection', timeless soul in 'Cold Wind In August', and blues-influenced tracks to open the record. Side one is barely 15 minutes long and far from wide-ranging. If it has a focus, it's jazz and blues, but compared to glorious first sides of other 1970s Morrison albums, this may seem underpowered. It has the largest Dr. John imprint and is almost a stand-alone project.

The album opens with the slow-building New Orleans blues warning that, if you can, 'You Gotta Make It Through The World'. The song takes its key line from the Mississippi Sheiks 1930 country/blues fiddle song 'Bootlegger's Blues', with its chorus of 'You better make it through the world if you can'.

Next is 'It Fills You Up': a dirty chugging tribute to the power of music, with few lyrics but an opening like a striptease. It has a great lead vocal and a complementary soul/gospel backing. This is the album track that shows Dr. John's involvement and influence the most.

Morrison saw 'The Eternal Kansas City' as the album's heart. Opening with the harmonies of the Anita Kerr Singers (Kerr, Anne Simmons, Danny Street, and future 'Postman Pat' voice actor Ken Barrie), it follows the last track neatly as another tribute to the power of song but channelled through the jazz and blues heritage of Kansas City, name-checking legends who arose from its 1930s scene: Billie Holiday, Charlie Parker, Count Basie, Lester Young, Jay McShann, and Jimmy Witherspoon, who sang on Morrison's *A Night in San Francisco* (1994): most notably 'Have You Ever Loved A Woman?' Morrison has said 'The Eternal Kansas City' was inspired by a dream after seeing the Birdland Park and Gardens in the Cotswolds, not too far from where he lived when recording the album in Oxfordshire. The visitor attraction made him think of writing a song about Charlie Parker, who was born in Kansas but for whom the New York club Birdland was set up in 1949. On the album, the song could've used more breathing space, and if extended to the length of the *Saint Dominic's Preview* side closers, it could've soared. But none of the *A Period of Transition* tracks makes it as far as six minutes.

Side two opens with a couple of older songs and closes with a brace of new ones. Though each was first put on tape years ago, the newly recorded versions of 'Joyous Sound' and 'Flamingos Fly' suited the album. They manage to fit the album dynamic, even though their composition and their upbeat pop go back quite a while: the latter to the Jackie De Shannon period. 'Flamingoes Fly' was even recorded by Sammy Hagar and first released on his 1976 debut album *Nine on a Ten Scale*.

'Joyous Sound' is the album's simplest song and had been through a few changes in concert over the years, beginning as gospel, and veering in emphasis between R&B, jazz and boogie. The track bounces along with the whole band funking it up, but – surprisingly – given the earlier version on *The Philosopher's Stone*, the backing singers don't enter until late in the track. It ends with one of the longest finales on a Morrison recording, as the brass section hold their notes, and the vocalists stretch out the final word 'again'.

While it changes the 'bluebirds fly' to 'Flamingos Fly', the next song owes a clear debt to the Kansas-set song from *The Wizard of Oz* 'Over The Rainbow', which it reworks as somewhere over the 'rooftops'; Morrison's song also references a 'clear blue sky' and hearing 'one time' in a lullaby about where flamingos fly. Like the Judy Garland classic, 'Flamingos Fly' intimates happiness somewhere in the distance. It will be reached as night turns to dawn, with the sound of the nightingale turning to that of the lark. Yet, the most fascinating line is a play on the nineteenth-century cowboy anthem, and also Kansas state song, 'Home On The Range': where the 'buffalo roam' and 'the deer and the antelope play'. Morrison swaps buffaloes for flamingos and antelopes for 'provincial angels', while still emphasizing that 'home' is where 'the deer' roam. This echoes the deer crossing by the lights in 'Snow In San Anselmo', and may also tap into ideas of the glimpse of a grazing deer representing a deep spiritual insight, which is the subject of the next song ('Heavy Connection'), into which Morrison interjects the 'rainbow' missing from his homage to Arlen and Harburg's 'Over The Rainbow' in 'Flamingos Fly'. The inspiration for the 'Flamingos Fly' song title lies in another connection to Peggy Lee and Morrison's touchstone year of 1956. In November of that year, Lee released a beautiful heartbreak song called 'Where Flamingos Fly': about her man being deported on a freighter back to his island home thousands of miles away.

'Heavy Connection' is another fine song. And though it doesn't hit the heights on the album, the recorded track hints at the power the composition could generate in concert when let loose. Morrison was reading psychoanalyst Carl Jung at the time, and the lyric implies that another possible title could've been 'Synchronicity'. Its key phrase 'From a whisper to a scream' imitates the track's building mood after the inspired brass introduction. The message of psychic identification transcending distance is staple Morrison subject matter: familiar from as far back as *Astral Weeks*. The lyric begins by mentioning musician Chris Kenner's 'Land Of 1000 Dances'. At the close, Morrison sings about not being able to stop a 'rainbow' in 'my soul': referencing the recurrent Gene Chandler hit 'Rainbow' (written by Curtis Mayfield). Mayfield's lyric focuses on a rainbow in the heart, not the soul. Morrison again references the song in his reworking of 'Real, Real Gone' on his 1990 album *Enlightenment*, singing at the very end about Gene Chandler saying 'There's a rainbow in my soul', after name-checking Sam Cooke, Wilson Pickett, Solomon Burke, and James Brown. Van performed the song live in later years, and in terms of recordings, it's used in the medley 'It's All In The Game/Make It Real One More Time' on the live 1994 album *A Night in San Francisco*.

The album ends strongly with 'Cold Wind In August' – a song Dr. John said was a 'crosscurrent from '40s to '70s music. It's like where Ray Charles left off. It's a real tearjerker that gets back to the basics of music'. The Ray Charles inspiration is clear – Morrison punctuating the beautiful and evocative song with allusions to the title of Arlen (again) and Mercer's 'Come Rain Or Come Shine', which Charles recorded in 1959. Presumably unconnected to the 1961 film *A Cold Wind in August*, it's a song of longing among the California pines: standing waiting for a lover in the garden in the cold and the rain. Appropriately, it's also a song of transition; summer pushing into autumn; September's chills in August. The lovesick lyric about shivers up and down the spine, seems to give a passing nod to 'Fever', which Morrison continued to perform in concert in 1977 and beyond: most often in a medley with 'Moondance' (see, for example, the 1990 video *Van Morrison The Concert,* recorded at New York's Beacon Theater in 1989). This tenuous link might even explain why 'Cold Wind In August' appeared as the B-side to 'Moondance', which Warner Bros. reissued as a single in September 1977. Two other singles were released from the album – an edited version of 'The Eternal Kansas City' in spring 1977 (UK only), and 'Joyous Sound' in July. The latter was the B-side of the former but had 'Mechanical Bliss' as its own flipside.

The album does mark a period of transition, but less of one from *Veedon Fleece* to *Wavelength* than one expressing Van's reconnection with his jazz, soul and blues heritage, and a return to the roots of his own music. In the 1980s, this original Morrison sound became a blend of Celtic, jazz, soul, balladry, blues, country and western, gospel, folk, classical and rock. The list seems long, but it is not difficult to pick out the influence of each of these traditions in his output in later decades.

In 1977 – despite the *health warning* of the title – critical reception for *A Period of Transition* was not good, and for most listeners, the album has never had a respected place in the Morrison canon. However, that reaction may partly be due to the record's length, the comparatively small number of songs (a couple of which had been kicking around for a while) and a brace of opening tracks that were a step away from the sound familiar to fans (partly due to the Dr. John collaboration). Taken in the round now, without the weight of expectation, it's obvious the album has good material, but also that these were quite possibly not the best versions of the songs. The compositions might've benefitted from the band taking them on the road for a couple of months first, and might've turned out better with different arrangements: on the record, the sound is muddy in comparison to later Morrison albums.

On the release of *A Period of Transition* in April 1977, Morrison gave a notorious interview to Nicky Horne on London's Capitol Radio, in which he refused to participate in the publicity game and talked about the album as nothing special, just product. Other promotional activities were mostly treated with similar disdain. In a way contradicting the very rationale for media exposure and PR, Morrison didn't wish to speak about his music to people with an agenda or with something of their own to promote, whether it be a music paper or a radio show. The album accordingly didn't sell well, and the relationship with Goldsmith didn't survive the aftermath. There was still uncertainty around questions like where Morrison would live (in the US or UK), whether there should be promotional gigs, and who should be in the touring band.

Morrison showed little inclination to go on the road, but when he did appear, it was special, and three fascinating film recordings were made. The first was at NBC's Burbank studios for *The Midnight Special* TV show, which aired on 22 April. Alongside backing singers and a band (including Dr. John on piano, Ollie Brown on bass, and John Platania back on guitar), Morrison played a 40-minute set featuring guest spots from Carlos Santana, Etta James, saxophonist Tom Scott and the show's host George Benson. Though the programme was widely broadcast, the only officially released song was 'Moondance': on a DVD of highlights from the *The Midnight Special* series. At over seven minutes, it has powerful singing from Van at the start, returning with a flourish at the finish. Otherwise, it's a showcase for the guests, each providing a solo, with Etta James scatting. Morrison ends the song by singing 'My face is wet' – a tribute to the James Brown version of 'Fever' which idiosyncratically ended with that repeated line. (As mentioned above, 'Moondance' was being coupled with 'Fever' in concert.)

During the set, four of the new album's best tracks were given superior outings ('Joyous Sound', 'Heavy Connection', 'Cold Wind In August', and 'The Eternal Kansas City'). But most unusual was the rendition of the Garner and Burke standard 'Misty' with George Benson on guitar. Morrison had played 'Misty' on the road as early as 1972, but the concert versions were faster – as at the Santa Monica gigs that year, where the song swings along at speed in a jazz style to follow 'I Will Be There'. Here, it's a two-man performance, with the guitarist dressed in white, standing beside a seated dark-clothed Morrison whose slow pace and phrasing Benson follows as the singer savours every word. (On Morrison's 2015 *Duets: Re-working the Catalogue* album, the pair sang 'Higher Than The World': the sublime opener of *Inarticulate Speech of the Heart* (1983).) A final observation to make is that on *The Midnight Special* performance, the opening of 'Heavy Connection' presages the beginning of 'Wavelength', when Morrison introduces it by singing 'This a song about... a heavy connection', pointing up the songs' similar theme. The performances of the four *A Period of Transition* songs were also shown on television in Europe and can be found in 1977 archive footage of the French programme *Jukebox*.

The second video was shot in early June for Granada's *So It Goes* television show in the UK, and aired in September. One of Morrison's few public live appearances since 1975, doing early and late shows at the 150-seat club Maunkberry's, in Mayfair. The cameras captured 'Venice USA' (later to appear on *Wavelength*) and a few other songs, including 'The Eternal Kansas City' and 'Joyous Sound'. Grainy footage shows Morrison comfortable in the small venue, seemingly relaxed and enjoying the material. He was joined by Roger Chapman, Brian Auger and other musicians for an hour-long second set featuring Sonny Boy Williamson II's 'Help Me', B. B. King's 'Rock Me Baby' and Bobby Bland's 'Turn On Your Love Light'.

The third video is from a short stint in June and features – after the previous two days' rehearsals – the final performance for the *Wonderland* TV show at the NOS Studios in Hilversum, after a 60-minute Vara studios Dutch FM radio broadcast. The shows feature some exploratory cover versions of Ray Charles' 'Hallelujah, I Love Her So', James Brown's 'I'll Go Crazy' and Blind Willie Johnson's 'Nobody's Fault But Mine' (which Led Zeppelin had just reworked on 1976's *Presence*). After warming up at Maunkberry's, the band experimented over three days. Some interesting selections were trialled at the rehearsals, including 'Johnny B. Goode' and 'The Tracks Of My Tears'. The widely-available video and audio recordings of the three days feature Dr. John on keyboards, Peter Van Hooke on drums, Mo Foster on bass, and Mick Ronson on guitar. The TV show includes four songs from *A Period of Transition,* with 'You Gotta Make It Through the World' transformed into more of a rock version after a warm-up of 'Joyous Sound'. Morrison takes to the piano for 'The Eternal Kansas City': its delicate skeleton discovered without the choir and brass ornamentation. The song's beauty appears as Morrison extends his vocal, drawing out the lyrics and even inserting a few lines from Dinah Shore's 'Buttons And Bows' – singing I'll love you 'where your friends don't tote a gun' and 'I'll love you in buckskin', which he was also to borrow for the end of the *Wavelength* track 'Hungry For Your Love'. Like several songs from *Hard Nose the Highway*, the *A Period of Transition* songs were revealing new layers in concert. But Morrison took the band no further and seemed more interested in pushing on to new material.

A European tour had been planned to promote *A Period of Transition*, but with something still playing Russian roulette with his thoughts, Morrison called it off: much to the frustration of his management. The year ended with him focusing on something more commercial while still being determined to produce the kind of music he wanted to make. As an indication, he performed on *The Midnight Special* again in October, tearing up a blistering six-and-a-half-minute version of 'Domino' with first-rate support from some solid North California musicians and backing singers. These were mostly those corralled into the group that had the huge 1976 hit 'Fooled Around And Fell In Love' with Elvin Bishop – who was hosting the show this time and had appeared on concert bills with Morrison as far back as 1970. The fact that Bishop – an original member of the Paul Butterfield Blues Band – was having a hit, certainly indicated the sales potential in turning to a more-contemporary sensibility. Morrison's next record would similarly be made with an eye on the charts, taking a few steps into the pop-rock arena, introducing synths and electric guitar solos on what would, on release, be his best-selling album to that point, reaching the top 30 on both sides of the Atlantic.

1978: Wavelength

Wavelength (1978)

Personnel:

Van Morrison: vocals, acoustic guitar, alto saxophone, piano, Fender Rhodes

Herbie Armstrong: acoustic guitar ('Checkin' It Out', 'Hungry For Your Love'; electric guitar ('Venice U.S.A.')

Mickey Feat: bass

Peter Bardens: synthesizer, Roland horns, keyboards

Garth Hudson: organ ('Take It Where You Find It'); accordion 'Venice U.S.A.'; synthesizer solo ('Kingdom Hall')

Bobby Tench: electric guitar, backing vocal

Peter Van Hooke: Drums

Kuma: bass ('Santa Fe/Beautiful Obsession', 'Take It Where You Find It')

Mitch Dalton: Spanish guitar ('Take It Where You Find It')

Ginger Blake, Laura Creamer, Linda Dillard: backing vocals

Producers: Van Morrison (with assistance from Mick Glossop, Bobby Tench, Peter Bardens)

All songs by Van Morrison except where stated

Recorded at The Manor, Oxfordshire, Spring 1978; overdubbed at Shangri-La Studio, L.A.

Release date: September 1978

Chart places: US: 28, UK: 27

Running time: 49:32

Tracklisting: Side One: 1. 'Kingdom Hall', 2. 'Checkin' It Out', 3. 'Natalia', 4. 'Venice U.S.A.', 5. 'Lifetimes'. Side Two: 1. 'Wavelength', 2. 'Santa Fe/Beautiful Obsession' (Jackie DeShannon/Morrison), 3. 'Hungry For Your Love', 4. 'Take It Where You Find It'

There were no gigs for the first nine months of 1978; the focus was firmly placed on producing a new album to bounce back from the lukewarm response accorded *A Period of Transition*, which had followed on from a critical failure to appreciate *Veedon Fleece*. The next record was going to be a completely different project, with high production values from the sound to the cover, a new band, more-catchy songs, and 15 minutes more music than the last album.

Released in September, *Wavelength* had Brooks Arthur back as engineer, bringing a slicker sound than previous records. The smooth production is a world away from *A Period of Transition*. That album arguably looked to the past, while the new one was the most contemporary sounding of Morrison's career. While rarely listed among his best albums, *Wavelength* has some essential music, and every track is worthy of fresh appraisal. The record signalled renewed energy after relatively fallow years, drawing rejuvenation both from recent influences and old music stations. After the last album left a downbeat impression, on release in September 1978, *Wavelength* spoke of renewal, love, enthusiasm and inspiration. It gave Van a new image at the time, but in retrospect, it may be best understood as a platform for the following albums of the next few years, which are often considered superior.

Unlike *A Period of Transition,* the new record showed an acute awareness of the changes going on in music in the late-1970s. The supporting musicians were a mix of old friends and recent acquaintances. Alongside rhythm guitarist, Herbie Armstrong – very familiar from the Manhattan Showband at Belfast's Plaza Mecca ballroom – was Bobby Tench, who'd jammed with Morrison at Maunkberry's the previous year. Tench provided distinctive backing vocals, and a contemporary electric guitar sound, with even a solo on the title track. One of the founding members of Camel, Peter Bardens – who'd played briefly with Them – brought with him the first synths used on a Morrison album. Bass on most tracks was played by Mickey Feat, and back on drums came 1974 stalwart Peter Van Hooke, who appeared on the next four albums before joining Mike + The Mechanics for a decade. Garth Hudson from The Band added another new keyboard dimension during overdubs at the group's Shangri-LA studio in Malibu.

Harvey Goldsmith had asked ex-Doors manager Bill Siddons to look after Morrison, but that relationship soon folded, and Bill Graham Management took over. After the release of *Wavelength*, the plan was for the first nationwide tour in four years. This was to be a long haul throughout October and November, with Morrison often performing at the top of his game in early gigs but needing a week off after the experience of playing at The Palladium in New York.

Van continued to prefer small venues where he could connect with an audience in the way his blues and jazz heroes had. Some great concert recordings came from the tour as a result. One of the more intimate of these – at The Bottom Line in New York on 1 November 1978 – was broadcast on several radio stations to great acclaim. Along with the gig at the Blue Note in Boulder, Morrison considered The Bottom Line to be the highlight of the tour. One moment fans have noticed from this concert is that in the *Wavelength* song 'Natalia' Morrison ends by singing phrases from another of his songs, the words 'turn around … hand on my shoulder', before adding 'You don't have to worry about the motion of the ocean'. (The same concert has 'Slim Slow Slider' inserted into 'Wild Night'.) Remarkably, the lines come from the *Hard Nose the Highway* track 'Autumn Song', which Van never plays in concert even though, as we know, he performed it at the RTE studio for his Irish TV special in 1973. At the end of 'Autumn Song', there are numerous softly-sung, almost spoken lines that rarely appear when the lyrics are transcribed, concluding with Morrison saying, 'I believe I've transcended myself child'. As noted earlier, Morrison also appended 'I believe I've transcended' to 'Astral Weeks' on the Hollywood Bowl version, so let's end by observing how 'Astral Weeks' talks about getting to the far side of the ocean by putting wheels in motion, even though the exact line 'Don't worry about the motion of the ocean' comes directly from James Brown's *Live at the Apollo, Volume II* (1968) version of 'It's a Man's, Man's, Man's World'.

The band for the gigs comprised the *Wavelength* players Tench, Armstrong, Bardens, Feat and Van Hooke, plus two backing singers: Anna Peacock and Katie Kissoon. The latter complemented the singing so well, she appeared on Van's next album. The full tour (with Irish and British legs) started in Santa Clara, California, on 30 September 1978, and after a long Christmas break, ended in mid-March 1979 in Newcastle upon Tyne. For the dates in the British Isles, sax players Pat Kyle and John Altman were added, plus fiddle player Toni Marcus. Marcus' importance can be likened to that of violinist Scarlet Rivera in Dylan's Rolling Thunder period, and her playing brought to the shows a romance and freedom that was looser than – but in many ways just as important as – the strings of the Caledonia Soul Orchestra. Taking on the musical director role, Altman added fresh song arrangements as the tour progressed, and the musicians became more relaxed: especially Marcus, who was the most extroverted performer. An accomplished jazz musician, Altman went on to a prestigious film-composing career, and he was already working on movie projects, including arranging and conducting 'Always Look On The Bright Side Of Life' for *Monty Python's Life of Brian* (1979).

An album recorded in the heart of England, with an ear to the sounds of 1978, *Wavelength* is a tribute to American ideas and old influences. It's a contemporary album steeped in memory more than in sentiments of the Studio 54 scene. The record starts with 'Kingdom Hall', which most people link back to Morrison's few visits with his mother to Jehovah's

Witnesses meetings in Belfast. This would've been one of the many formative scenes of communal singing that Van experienced, though not normally of dancing. 'Kingdom Hall' is however a song about having a party, having a ball, and dancing like you've never done before. The lyric description seems more like a local Gospel Hall meeting than one held by most Jehovah's Witnesses congregations. There is a choir and bells ringing, but no mention of worship in 'Kingdom Hall', and the picture painted is either of a full-on Pentecostal party or simply a liberating and uninhibited Gospel Hall dance.

Overall, *Wavelength* is an album with hooks and simple rhymes, starting with the 'Hey, liley, liley' chant of the choir at the 'Kingdom Hall' ('Hey Liley, Liley Lo' was a 1957 skiffle hit). This is followed by a chorus of 'do do do's with Tench's electric guitar lines while Morrison extols the virtues of the good rockin' music. This was the album's third single (US only), 'Wavelength' being the first, with its own 'do do do's. The second single, 'Natalia' repeats the song title's opening syllable to the point of chanting, adding to the ever-growing subset of 'na na na' songs (headed by 'Land Of 1000 Dances' and 'Hey Jude'). This, however, is not a tongue-tied 'Cyprus Avenue' repetition because Morrison has always judiciously used the blues legends' stammer effect, which was well-known from songs like John Lee Hooker's 'Stuttering Blues' (1953). (Both Hooker and B. B. King had stutters in early life, and used singing to help overcome them). 'Venice U.S.A.' has a Bo Diddley beat and a chorus that goes 'Dum diddly, dum dum, diddy, diddy, dah, dah'. Phrasing of this type was used in myriad songs, ranging from Billy Boy Arnold's 'Diddy Diddy Dum Dum' to the The Exciters' 'Doo Wah Diddy Diddy' – so successfully covered by Manfred Mann, and presumably inspired by Blind Blake and Bo Diddley songs about the mythical place 'Diddy Wah Diddy'. Like in the Manfred Mann hit, Morrison makes his ditty a song within the song; something sung while walking along: 'Sing a song, goes like this'.

In other words, the *Wavelength* tracks – and especially the singles – were to an extent, framed as pop songs and aimed at the charts. This is feel-good music, and several other tracks made excellent radio-friendly cuts – 'Hungry For Your Love', 'Checkin' It Out', and 'Lifetimes': the latter two used as B-sides. In 1978, the six songs mentioned so far were the *Wavelength* songs that Morrison played live.

'Checkin' It Out' is one of only two *Wavelength* recordings to feature brass – Morrison playing alto sax, as on the title track. Nestled between 'Kingdom Hall' and 'Natalia', it has a lyric about connection and reconciliation, like many other songs on the record. It also draws in the idea of guiding spirits and meditation, evoking another aspect to the album's theme of wavelengths – linked to radio, communion, and connection across continents. It ends with an observation of how you meditate and then 'come back'. This returns in the title track with the Voice of America calling 'come back': of which more later.

'Natalia' is a catchy slice of upbeat pop revelling in reconnecting with a lover. It brings together romance tropes, focusing on walking and talking on a magical summer night. The song speaks of being 'hungry' for his lover's kiss, which links 'Natalia' to the album's final love song 'Hungry For Your Love'. Thematically, 'Natalia' matches 'Venice U.S.A.', with its own scene of lovers in a restaurant who walk along to see the ships sailing in. The imagery is distinctly familiar – all the streets are wet with rain, the singer's tears are filled with joy, the ships can be seen coming into the harbour. It's a song of leaving and memory, with Garth Hudson's accordion playing mellow and bright: adding to the impression of being at the harbourside.

While it has a more complex lyric, 'Lifetimes' continues the water-and-song association. Morrison creates a parallel between the silence of listening to the music inside and hearing the boatman singing far across the water: inspiring a response in heart and soul. A sense of death and rebirth anchors the song in a meditation on journeying into silence; of Charon taking the Tennysonian traveller across the river Styx into the mystic: 'I hope to see my pilot face to face/When I have crost the bar'. The track has impressive backing vocals – the male bass of Tench suggesting the boatman, and the female harmonies of Blake, Creamer, and Dillard intimating the river flow. 'Lifetimes' begins by observing how the river answers the meditative questioner. The protagonist is the river of time, who speaks while the angel of the night's wings envelop the silent meditator, banishing doubt. The intriguing imagery echoes the poem on the back cover of *Astral Weeks*, with its line about seeing 'you' coming from across the river.

Opening side two is 'Wavelength' – a Morrison classic which Dave Marsh put at 253 in *The Heart of Rock & Soul*: his book of the 1001 greatest singles ever made. This title track features Tench's radio-friendly guitar-playing, providing a joyous, soaring solo. The song is the album lynchpin – a paean to the power of radio and to the sound of rhythm and blues calling across the Atlantic. 'Wavelength' also invokes 'Brown Eyed Girl' in its reference to a lover in the grass, highlighting the line in Morrison's hit single that was censored on American radio back in 1967 and replaced with an edit insert taken from the first verse. The 'Wavelength' lyric emphasises the impact of hearing songs like Ray Charles' soul-defining 'Come Back Baby', and it's a hymn to connection – to finding the wavelength for a lover or for a radio station like Luxembourg, Athlone, Hilversum, Hellvetia, Budapest or the American Forces Network (AFN), as Van later lists them in the *Enlightenment* song 'In The Days Before Rock 'n' Roll'. He's emphasised in interviews that the song is not about FM radio but an old radio service run by the United States government. In 1979, he told *Melody Maker*: 'It's actually about Europe because that's where the station was. It came out of Frankfurt, and the first time I ever heard Ray Charles was on the Voice of America. We tried to get a tape recording of the Voice of America to put on the front of that track, but it didn't work out'.

'Santa Fe' is an older song, written back in 1973 with Jackie DeShannon, and another with a restaurant setting. It describes the Wordsworthian pleasure of emotion recollected in tranquillity – recalling the feeling of connecting with someone over food and wine, or simple memories of the joy of nature from the mountain top down to the evening breeze and the sea. The idea that a memory – like, for Morrison, a returning train – draws you back into intensely felt experiences segues into 'Beautiful Obsession', which itself dates back to at least 1971. The song continues the US fascination that the overall album implies, evoking the American West in particular, with a closing request to 'let the cowboy ride'. Morrison used to sing this line back in Boston in 1968, no doubt drawing in numerous echoes of everything Western, from the Lone Ranger to Marty Robbins's 'Ride, Cowboy Ride'. Bob Seger seemingly picked up Morrison's line, much rarer than might be thought, to rework as 'Let the cowboys ride' in his 1980 hit single 'Against The Wind'.

The album's last love song, 'Hungry for your Love' is a fine addition to the list of 1970s Morrison classics that already included 'Crazy Love', 'Tupelo Honey', 'Warm Love', and less-famous favourites like 'I'll Be Your Lover, Too' and 'Come Here My Love'. Another song about getting connected, it adds the cowboy line 'I'll love you in buckskin' from the otherwise anti-Western 'Buttons And Bows'. Morrison would've known many versions of the song, recorded by artists such as Evelyn Knight, Gene Autry, and Dinah Shore. It was written for Bob Hope to sing in the 1948 film *The Paleface*, which earned it an Oscar for best song. As mentioned earlier, Morrison would add the 'love you in buckskin' line

DECADES | *Van Morrison in the 70s*

to other songs in performance (such as 'The Eternal Kansas City' in the Hilversum Wonderland show from June 1977), along with that other 'Buttons And Bows' line saying I'll love you 'where your friends don't tote a gun'.

A song that gestated over several years, 'Take It Where You Find It' is another exemplary lyric about perceiving through the eyes of a child, and – with echoes of everything from 'Midnight Special' to 'I Shall Be Released' – seeing a shining light. It begins with the contemplation of liberty by thinkers and poets staring at the stars at the edge of the sea, imagining a new world. The bridge section speaks of dreams lost and found in America. But this is a song of new purpose, about finding change in the self through inspiration – close your eyes and leave behind the world of worry in order to awaken to a new world: a sense of which is conjured by Mitch Dalton's Spanish guitar. The song has a five-part structure and reaches for a grandeur absent elsewhere on the album; the music and theme of exploration building from an early visionary glimpse of possibility to a guiding light taking the singer towards his personal and artistic destiny. Again, the sentiment of discovery can be found earlier on the record: another thematic link. The connection between worlds, physical or metaphysical, echoes throughout Morrison's work, finding expression in many songs – perhaps most interestingly in 'That's Entrainment' on *Keep It Simple* (2008), which draws on the concept of entrainment to articulate what Morrison aims for in his music. He explained on the Lost Highway records website: 'Entrainment is really what I'm getting at in the music ... It's kind of when you're in the present moment ... with no past or future'.

Norman Seeff's *Wavelength* cover photograph blends a monochrome portrait of a casual half-smiling Morrison seated against a plain background with some pastel lines drawn on top. This is clearly an artful, staged but contemporary studio shot. The only thing in common with the cover of *A Period of Transition* is the cigarette. The sleeve insert is again monochrome: white lyrics on a black background. *Wavelength* was to be Morrison's last album for Warner Bros..

The trek across the USA in the closing months of 1978 was Morrison's first large-scale tour in four years. It brought him back to public attention, and after the West Coast dates, the shows took in much of the country, including Dallas, Detroit, Boston, Washington, and New York. In early November, Morrison performed 'Wavelength' on *Saturday Night Live* at NBC studios. With a two-night booking in Toronto along the way, the

North American leg ended in early December back at San Francisco's Winterland.

However, there was one other notable performance in 1978 – not in concert, but back in London at Advision Studios, where Morrison laid down a vocal on Frank Zappa's 'Dead Girls of London' – probably the hardest rock track Morrison ever appeared on. Zappa wrote the song with violinist Lakshminarayana Shankar. With blistering electric guitar and violin interplay, it's a bitter song about striking out with the 'little robot queens' from the disco at the exclusive Tramp nightclub in Mayfair. Zappa explained in a 1980 interview with Michael Davis for *Record Review*:

> I was sitting in the studio scribbling some words down when I got this phone call out of nowhere. It was Van Morrison, who was shopping for a new label in Europe. I don't know Van very well, but I asked him to stop by the studio and see if he'd sing this song. He walked in and took one take: 15 minutes was all it took. He came in, sang the song and left.

Though Zappa and Morrison were both still contracted to Warner Bros., neither was to be for much longer and, with Morrison's vocal, the label wouldn't sanction releasing the track on Zappa's own label given their differences. Zappa recorded a new version, sharing vocals with Ike Willis, and put the song out on Shankar's Zappa Records album *Touch Me There* (1979). Morrison's vocal version remained locked away for over 30 years until it was officially released as part of the download-only compilation *The Frank Zappa AAAFNRAAAAAM Birthday Bundle 2011*. Whether or not 'Dead Girls Of London' is thought to be an important Morrison track, it was certainly in stark contrast to the genuflections to synths on *Wavelength*. The song is Zappa's attack on the disco culture, and by the time Vicky Blumenthal's backing vocal arrives, it's far more in tune with the new wave spirit of the times, despite Phil Palmer's searing guitar-hero contribution. Morrison's exclamatory vocal is like nothing on his own album and perfectly matches the incendiary hard rock electricity screeching through the track.

1979: Into the Music

Into the Music (1979)

Personnel:

Van Morrison: harmonica, rhythm guitar, vocals

Peter Van Hooke: drums

Kurt Wortman: drums ('Troubadours')

David Hayes: bass

Ry Cooder: slide Guitar ('Full Force Gale')

Herbie Armstrong: guitar, backing vocal

Pee Wee Ellis: saxophone, arrangements

Mark Isham: trumpet, flugelhorn, piccolo trumpet, Arrangements

Zakir Hussain: tabla ('Bright Side Of The Road', 'Stepping Out Queen')

Mark Jordan: keyboards

Katie Kissoon: backing vocals

Toni Marcus: mandolin, violin, viola, Stroh viola

Robin Williamson: penny whistle ('Troubadours', 'Rolling Hills')

John Allair: Hammond organ ('And the Healing Has Begun')

Producers: Van Morrison, Mick Glossop

All songs by Van Morrison unless stated

Recorded at The Record Plant, Sausalito, early-1979

Release date: August 1979

Chart places: US: 43, UK: 21

Running time: 49:30

Tracklisting: Side One: 1. 'Bright Side Of The Road', 2. 'Full Force Gale', 3. 'Stepping Out Queen', 4. 'Troubadours', 5. 'Rolling Hills', 6. 'You Make Me Feel So Free'. Side Two: 1. 'Angeliou', 2. 'And The Healing Has Begun', 3. 'It's All In The Game' (Dawes, Sigman), 4. 'You Know What They're Writing About'

No longer feeling Warner Bros. were giving him sufficient support, Morrison signed a record deal with Polydor in spring 1979. With a permanent move to Europe still on the cards, a 21-date Britain/Ireland tour in the first half of 1979 was an opportunity to take the show to new places. One of these venues was Whitla Hall in Belfast, and the concerts sold out in half an hour. The return home also prompted the making of the documentary *Van Morrison in Ireland*. Directed by Mike Radford in February 1979 (but released two years later), the documentary was mostly comprised of concert footage, with snippets of life on the tour bus and Morrison revisiting sites in Belfast. Songs included from the Whitla Hall perfomances are 'Moondance', 'Moonshine Whiskey', 'Tupelo Honey', 'Wavelength', 'Saint Dominic's Preview', John Lee Hooker's 'Don't Look Back' (on the first Them album), 'I've Been Working', 'Gloria', and 'Cyprus Avenue'. Sound was overseen by Morrison's resident engineer of the late-1970s, Mick Glossop, and camera work was in part conducted by now-legendary cinematographer Roger Deakins. The documentary omits the concert outings of 'And it Stoned Me', 'Into the Mystic', 'Crazy Love', 'Checkin' it Out', and 'Caravan'.

After the tour, Morrison stayed on with Herbie Armstrong in the Cotswolds village of Epwell, and rented a house in a nearby Oxfordshire village. Most of the next album *Into the Music* was written at this time, in the English countryside, though Morrison returned to Sausalito to record the songs in early summer.

Another release clocking in at virtually 50 minutes – almost identical in length to *Wavelength* – *Into the Music* is the first album to feature some key Morrison collaborators in the same band. There's not only the continued presence of Herbie Armstrong and Peter Van Hooke but the return of David Hayes and Mark Jordan. There's also the important introduction of session musician Mark Isham, and Pee Wee Ellis: an acquaintance of Isham's who'd played with James Brown. Morrison discards Bardens' synths for *Into the Music,* and the influence of Isham and Ellis shapes a brass sound almost completely absent from *Wavelength*. Isham later became a prolific film composer working on high-profile Hollywood productions and receiving an Oscar nomination for the soundtrack to *A River Runs Through It*. Becoming musical director and horn arranger on the next album, *Common One*, Ellis worked with Morrison regularly over the next 20 years, through to a final appearance on *Back on Top* (1999).

These musicians formed the core of Morrison's band over the following years. Though it changed on the next two LPs, the result on this album was a soulful, barrelling folk rock. The sound is introduced on 'Bright Side Of The Road' – Morrison's life-affirming response to James Carr's 1967 hit 'The Dark End Of The Street' – while the album concludes in a more-mellow vein with a lush and spacious reinterpretation of Tommy Edwards' 'It's All In The Game'. David Hayes commented to *Uncut*'s Tom Pinnock in 2015: 'The album has an English folk feel, but also a sunny side, because we recorded it at the Record Plant in Sausalito … Van was having a good time making the record. It felt like a new beginning. It was cut in about four days, all live, but he worked a little bit more on the arrangements with us'.

After the alternative directions of the previous two albums, *Into the Music* is indeed a watershed; the stepping stone into Morrison's work for the rest of the century – during which he rediscovered a forward-looking purpose and conviction that seemed a little lacking on *A Period of Transition* and *Wavelength*, adorned though they were with great songs. *Into the Music* introduced a compelling new sound from a band that could stand comparison with the Caledonia Soul Orchestra, and a unity of vision across lyrics focused on kinds of love: natural and protective, transcendent and spiritual, regained and redemptive.

Into the Music was released in August 1979. The 2008 remaster featured longer versions of 'Steppin' Out Queen' and 'Troubadours'. Additionally, *The Philosopher's Stone* has the outtake 'Stepping Out Queen Part 2', and a different version of 'Bright Side Of The Road' with more-prominent harmonica and a more-loose vocal approach, but without the brass section, Hussain's table, or Kissoon's vocals.

'Bright Side Of The Road' was the album's opening track and its first single. Released in September 1979 and peaking at 63, it was Morrison's only top 100 UK single of the 1970s. With a great harmonica break in the middle, it has an infectious rhythm and an optimistic lyric. It can be placed in the long line of new-dawn/bright-light lyrics Morrison had employed in various songs since 'Brand New Day' on *Moondance*, though now with the added sense of mortality and precious time passing that became commonplace in his later work. 'Bright Side Of The Road' is the first track to include tabla virtuoso Hussain, who played with John McLaughlin in the fusion band Shakti, and also with L. Shankar, who played on Zappa's 'Dead Girls Of London' in 1978. Kissoon and Armstrong supplied complementary backing vocals, while Morrison undertook his own Louis Armstrong impression towards the end. The song lyric reprises the idea of reunited lovers, which is also woven throughout much of the rest of the album. Dan Penn (co-writer of 'The Dark End Of The Street') covered 'Bright Side Of The Road' on *Vanthology* in 2003, and Colombian pop star Shakira performed it at Barack Obama's inauguration.

Two *Into the Music* songs reflect Van's interest in a pantheistic spirituality or Christian mysticism; he sings of finding 'sanctuary in the Lord' when lifted up like a 'full force gale', and of reading his Bible among the 'rolling hills' of the Cotswolds. This mix of nature with a reverent sensibility was to characterise Morrison's output for much of the 1980s, without ever veering towards the austere sanctimony of Dylan's

Christian albums. On 'Full Force Gale' – an album highlight, released in some territories as a single – Ry Cooder's slide guitar solo adds to the full band sound of rhythm and brass section, string accompaniment brought to full expression in Marcus' swirling fiddle-playing, and Kissoon's sweet distinctive backing vocals. Morrison creates a kind of pastoral gospel, to which he returned on future albums. The 1997 UK single of 'The Healing Game' contains a new version of 'Full Force Gale' as one of its four tracks. This stately but swinging take nearly 20 years after the original begins with the brass section rather than violin and drums, but is equally affecting, with Georgie Fame's Hammond and Brian Kennedy's shadow-singing (repeating each line Morrison sings) to the fore.

'Steppin' Out Queen' highlights Hussain's tabla to more striking effect than on 'Bright Side Of The Road', and develops Morrison's interplay with Kissoon: her call-and-response deepening into new refrains. In the fadeout, Kissoon recites four times the invitation to come into the garden, sit and talk and look at the flowers. An antecedent is Balfe's 'Come Into The Garden, Maud' – famously sung by John McCormack and based on Tennyson's poem 'Song For Maud', which speaks of the 'Queen rose of the rosebud garden of girls'.

'Steppin' Out Queen' is one of three related recordings, and taken together, they suggest a longer track might've emerged. First is the version called 'Steppin' Out Queen (Alternative Take)' included on the 2008 *Into the Music* remaster. This seven-minute take has no mention of the 'garden', focusing instead on the 'It's just a windfall away' refrain. A slower more-acoustic take without the brass, it seems to more suit a recording that might've been envisaged as 'Part 1' to the third version: the four-and-half-minute 'Stepping Out Queen Part 2' on *The Philosopher's Stone*, again lacking a horn section. 'Part 2' includes the garden invitation missing from the 'Alternative Take', but then moves beyond this to the desire for a more physical relationship. There's also an intriguing opening monologue to 'Part 2' – anticipatory at times of Dylan's 'Brownsville Girl', and reminiscent of the spoken-word sections on side two of *Into the Music*: most noticeably 'And The Healing Has Begun'. 'Part 2' has more room for Marcus' violin, and the track builds from a slow acoustic opening to a whirling climax.

'Steppin' Out Queen' could've been an epic to rival 'It's All In The Game/You Know What They're Writing About'. The *Into the Music* version appears to be a compressed version of the story in the other two songs but utilising the full band. Though starting as a tribute to a lover going out to a party, it joins the lineage of Morrison's songs about gardens and revelations, which extend from *Astral Weeks* to the magisterial 'In the Garden' on *No Guru, No Method, No Teacher* (1986) and beyond.

With traditional instruments, 'Troubadours' celebrates the strolling medieval antecedents to tourers and buskers, and is appropriately declarative in its sound palette. Mark Isham explained to Uncut's Tom Pinnock: 'I was a specialist in the piccolo trumpet, and Van said that he wanted that 'Penny Lane' sound on 'Troubadours'. He had left a hole in that track for it, he could hear it, so I improvised a part and it worked really well'. There are also starring parts for Ellis' sax and Marcus' fiddle, but the memorable impression is made by the pageantry of the brass fanfare. The Incredible String Band's Robin Williamson also features on penny whistle, and is retained for the next track – the mystical jig 'Rolling Hills': about being in the countryside, at peace with humanity, God and work. Williamson – a reader of Celtic literature and writers like L. Ron Hubbard and Alice Bailey – provided fuel for Morrison's interest in spiritual and esoteric writings. Williamson was also the writer of 'For Mr Thomas', which Morrison recorded in the early-1980s and included on *The Philosopher's Stone*.

Side one finishes with the magnificent 'You Make Me Feel So Free' – B-side of the US 'Full Force Gale'. The closing track provides a fitting end to a series of strong feel-good songs fusing Morrison's R&B roots with the pop sensibility of *Wavelength*, refracted through acoustic instruments. With a funky horn arrangement and a wonderful Pee Wee Ellis solo with shades of the melody of 'What's Going On' (as Morrison acknowledges in concert versions), the recording adds to a rich heritage of similarly-titled tributes, from 'You Make Me Feel So Young' to 'You're Gonna Make Me Lonesome When You Go'.

Side two is a suite similar to that on side two of *Hard Nose the Highway*. Where those songs emphasised nature, this cycle focuses on the curative power of romantic and sensual love, prefiguring Marvin Gaye's 'Sexual Healing' by a few years. The lessons on how to live studded throughout side one, are taken into lessons on how to love on side two. Epitomising this love theme, 'Angeliou' is about finding a new lover in springtime in Paris. It describes a heavy connection with another soul seeker – someone who's been on an inner 'search and a journey' just like the singer's. Morrison declares he has a story too, but because it has no words, he sings the title again, which is a highly uncommon – if not invented – variant on Angela or Angelou that suggests the sound of a word is more important than any meaning (as happens so often in Morrison's writing). Even so, the sense of someone angelic almost magically appearing before the singer, adds to the lyric's epiphanic aspect (compare 'Maria' in *West Side Story*, for example). Starting with piano and guitar, the other instruments are introduced one by one before – following a couple of affirmative shouts – Morrison announces the name of his new love.

With its references to avenues, a summer dress and Easter bonnet, 'And The Healing Has Begun' continues the impression of a glorious Paris springtime. It also recalls 'Steppin' Out Queen' by mentioning making music under the stars for 'hours and hours'. The opening lines talk about singing songs from way back, and the immediate reference is to the 1948 film *Easter Parade* and 'We're A Couple Of Swells' in the repeated reference 'We'll walk up the Avenue'. The healing game here is one of love and romance as much as music and sex. Morrison returns to the subject first used in 'He Ain't Give You None' of 'jelly roll', which he situates on the backstreets, most prominently on *Astral Weeks* and its career-defining Avenue. Morrison read Alan Lomax's book *Mister Jelly Roll* back in the 1950s and heard the term associated with Jelly Roll Morton, who played piano in a brothel at age 14. Morrison would've also encountered the expression in songs by Barbecue Bob (Robert Hicks), in Billy Eckstine's 'Jelly, Jelly' (which appeared in some 1990s Morrison concerts), and in Charlie Mingus' 'My Jelly-Roll Soul' (which Morrison reworked as 'gypsy soul' in 'Into The Mystic'). 'And The Healing Has Begun' mentions Muddy Waters, and no doubt there's a record like 'Rock Me' or 'I Just Want to Make Love To You' in mind. But another context is also the fact that 'Muddy Water Blues' was the B-side of Jelly Roll Morton's first record back in 1923. Additionally, Morrison drops in a James Brown allusion, suddenly declaring 'I can't stand myself' – a reference to Brown's 1967 hit 'I Can't Stand Myself (When You Touch Me)', which has a parallel narrative about a strong sexual connection (and Pee Wee Ellis was in the band that recorded Brown's *I Can't Stand Myself When You Touch Me* album). 'And the Healing Has Begun' has a stately grace as each of the musicians again begin to play after an acoustic guitar opening, followed by drums and bass. Kissoon is stood down while Toni Marcus takes control of the melody, circling around Morrison's vocal. Eschewing the brass, John Allair adds a Hammond organ part alongside Jordan's piano. After Garth Hudson introduced the Hammond organ on the previous album, Marin-County stalwart Allair became a constant over the next four albums, as

Morrison looked forward to forging his new Celtic folk and soul sound after the singularity of *Common One* (1980).

Acknowledging once more the tradition from which Morrison's songwriting comes, the next track is his heartfelt rendition of the classic about the dating game 'It's All In The Game'. In the 1950s, songwriter Carl Sigman added words to the melody written before the Great War by future US Vice President Charles Dawes. Against a gentle drum rhythm, the strings (especially Marcus' viola) seize the music from the outset, and for a third time in a row, the track is beyond the 40-second mark before the vocal starts. As on each of side two's songs, the artistry especially lies in the playoff between sound and silence, as quiet and crescendo take their turns to point up contemplative space and soaring emotion. Peter Van Hooke explained to Uncut's Pinnock:

> It was intuitive communication. 'It's All In The Game' was actually much longer than that, it was edited down. There was a sense of great achievement from everybody when we finished the take. It happened because everyone was listening and ready to have a collective experience, and Van was willing to really open himself up.

Knowing that an unedited version exists adds to the sense that Morrison just had too much good music to fit on the album, with longer versions of several tracks in the can. 'It's All In The Game' segues into 'You Know What They're Writing About', and the brass instruments soar over the vocal as the song builds to a climax before dropping out to create space once more, at times leaving only the piano or violin to point up the silence around them. The two tracks merge seamlessly, and share so much that they constitute the kind of portmanteau Morrison had essayed so many times in concert. As a hush descends at the end, he whispers that he wants his love to meet him one more time – drawing a link from a recent lover like 'Angeliou' back to the girl in the hollow, playing a 'new game' by the river, meeting beside the water and beneath the pylons.

In a 1979 interview at London's Royal Garden Hotel, Morrison told Chris Welch for *Melody Maker*: 'Music is like a healing thing, and we're all being healed. I'm being healed. That's what I know, what I feel. People go to a rock 'n' roll show and they come away feeling better. Any kind of art or music is involved in healing'. Morrison was expressing his own view, but also that found in the musical and spiritual teachings of Cyril Scott, among others. Composer, poet and spiritualist Scott advocated that religion is a search for self-knowledge and the divinity within, because God exists in every living thing. He also thought great music had an esoteric, mystical effect that precipitated change. Morrison became indebted to Scott's 1933 book *Music: Its Secret Influence Throughout the Ages*, and the belief in healing through music and knowledge became a foundational concept on Morrison's 1980s albums.

The side-two suite also signals Morrison's spiritual move from America to Europe, where he was to perform more, and also soon come to live. The second half of 1979 was notable for his first significant solo tour of continental Europe – taking in France, Belgium, Norway, Sweden, the Netherlands, and Denmark, before an unusual headlining spot at the Edinburgh Rock Festival on 1 September with The Chieftains, Talking Heads, Steel Pulse, and The Undertones. Gigs followed back in the States across September and October before the final show of the decade took place at Berkeley on 21 October. It was broadcast on *King Biscuit Flower Hour* – an American syndicated radio show that – from 1973 on – featured concert performances from various rock acts.

After the years of searching, Morrison was now on a roll – indeed, for the next 30 years, he'd go no more than two years without recording an album. In the days of vinyl, there was frequently more material than could be included on an LP. Other tracks from the *Into the Music* sessions to see the light of day include the lolloping blues standard 'I'm Ready', which was issued in 1999 on the principal 'Back On Top' single, along with a version of the traditional folk marching song 'John Brown's Body': slated to appear on *The Philosopher's Stone* but replaced later on. An alternative CD single of 'Back On Top' contained the 1979 track 'Sax Instrumental No. 1' (which pointed towards instrumental tracks of the early-1980s) and a live version of 'Tell Me'. Other outtakes from the sessions were 'Spirit' (recorded in a new version on the next album), 'Quality Street' (a version of which appeared later on *Hymns to the Silence*), and an update on the 1973 single with Jackie DeShannon 'Sweet Sixteen'. More obscure recordings were 'Are you Ready?', an instrumental called 'Sacramento' and the simple 'Blues Jam'.

There are two other releases associated with 1979. The official limited-edition promotional album *Live at the Roxy* was issued in January 1979 for the Warner Bros. Music Show tape and disc series. It was recorded the previous November with Katie Kissoon and Anne Peacock on vocals, Peter Bardens on keyboards, Bobby Tench on electric guitar, Peter Van Hooke and Mickey Feat on drums, and Herbie Armstrong on acoustic and electric guitars. Side one has 'Brown Eyed Girl', 'Wavelength', 'And it Stoned Me', 'Checkin' It Out', 'Hungry For Your Love' and 'Kingdom Hall', while side two has 'Crazy Love' performed by Kissoon, 'Tupelo Honey', 'Caravan' and 'Cyprus Avenue'. Two of the tracks, 'Wavelength' and 'Kingdom Hall', appeared on the 2008 *Wavelength* deluxe edition.

Also, an unofficial live DVD and double-CD recorded at the New Jersey gig on 6 October 1979 was released in 2012: *Live at the Capitol Theatre Passaic NJ 1979*. Though the band are in fine form, the sound is variable to poor, and often muddy and muffled. The setlist has a healthy selection from the new album and a good sprinkling of past favourites but is without anything from *Veedon Fleece, Astral Weeks* or *A Period of Transition*.

The tracklist was 'Kingdom Hall', 'Bright Side Of The Road', 'Here Comes The Night', 'Into The Mystic', 'You Make Me Feel So Free', 'Warm Love', 'Call Me Up In Dreamland', 'It's All In The Game/You Know What They're Writing About', 'Ain't Nothin' You Can Do', 'Angeliou', 'Full Force Gale', 'Moondance', 'Wavelength', 'Tupelo Honey', 'I've Been Working', 'Troubadours', 'Brown Eyed Girl', and 'Gloria'. 'Moonshine Whiskey' was also performed on the night. The band was the core of the studio players, with a couple of returning notables. Peter Van Hooke on drums, David Hayes on bass, John Platania and Herbie Armstrong on guitar, Pete Wingfield on keyboards, Mark Isham on trumpet, Toni Marcus on violin, Katie Kissoon on vocals and Pee Wee Ellis on saxophone.

Released on the Mercury label outside America, *Into the Music* was Morrison's first album for Polygram. It mostly garnered positive reviews, with many critics rating it as one of his best and often highlighting the song cycle on side two. The cover shot was a blue-and-white close-up of Morrison closed-eyed and concentrating on the music. A guitar strap is just visible. The Norman Seeff shot is repeated on the back cover in brown and white. Seeff's website has a similar photograph from the same session – showing Morrison posed almost identically, this time with guitar neck and microphone visible, placing the image in a studio setting. This alternative image was used for the cover of *The Essential Van Morrison* (2015), with the background blacked out.

Into the Music marks the end of the 1970s but the start of Morrison's overt interest in, and expression of, a pantheism that was to inform his work in the 1980s. There is renewed purpose and a new energy to the music, which evolved into a different sound over the next few albums as the European influence grew and Morrison's R&B roots were integrated into a soulful fusion of jazz and Celtic folk.

Afterwards: Common One

Common One (1980)

Personnel:
Van Morrison: guitar, harmonica, vocals
Mick Cox: lead guitar
Peter Van Hooke: drums
David Hayes: bass, backing vocals
Mark Isham: trumpet, flugelhorn
John Allair: Hammond organ, piano, Fender Rhodes, backing vocals
Herbie Armstrong: acoustic and rhythm guitar, backing vocals
Pee Wee Ellis: saxophone, flute
Pete Brewis: backing vocals ('Satisfied')
Producers: Van Morrison, Henry Lewy
Recorded at Super Bear Studios, Nice, France, 11-19 February 1980
All songs by Van Morrison
Release date: August 1980
Chart places: US: 73, UK: 53
Running time: 55:01
Tracklisting:Side One: 1. 'Haunts Of Ancient Peace', 2. 'Summertime In England',
3. 'Satisfied'. Side Two: 1. 'Wild Honey', 2. 'Spirit', 3. 'When Heart Is Open'

Before the 1970s came *Astral Weeks*: the album most fans and critics point to as Morrison's finest achievement. But it was a commercial failure at the time, and the critics simply didn't get it in 1968 either. It took the advocacy of an influential few, the success of *Moondance,* and changing tastes in music, for most listeners to understand that there was an underappreciated work of genius to be discovered. This became a pattern for several other Morrison albums, of which *Veedon Fleece* remains the prime example.

In 1980 came *Common One*: another brilliant and misunderstood record. Morrison has called it a favourite among his own albums: 'It's a mixture of different components – a bit of funk, blues, gospel. It's quite a fusion, and plus, I seemed to tap into something, and that particular band seemed to have a rapport'. Released to a music industry that was riding a new wave, *Common One* appeared in stores alongside debut albums by U2 and The Pretenders while the music press heralded the *avant garde* epitomised by Talking Heads' *Remain in Light* and Joy Division's *Closer.* In terms of vaunted performers from the 1970s, there was the huge success of established artists producing big sellers, such as Stevie Wonder's *Hotter than July* and Bruce Springsteen's *The River*.

Recorded in February 1980, *Common One* itself had nothing in common with the music scene. The album's sheer originality and freedom baffled critics who found its fusion of styles incomprehensible, its emphasis on spirit unpalatable, and the length of its tracks indulgent. Writing in the *NME*, Paul du Noyer filed it under 'muzak'. Record buyers largely shunned it too, and the album failed to make the top 50 on either side of the Atlantic. But 40 years have changed a lot of opinions. As the closing track states, people change 'When Heart Is Open', yet it's a travesty that only by listening to a range of other artists – from Steve Reich and Brian Eno to Miles Davis and The Waterboys – did critical opinion find a way to appreciate the beauty of an album like *Common One*. Not that the record sounds much like the work of any other artist. With a diversity far greater than usually noted, it starts and ends with gentle meditations in 'Haunts Of Ancient Peace' and 'When Heart Is Open'. The intervening four tracks are varied and complex, sharing only their variety of sound in common, with each song rising to melodic swells and subsiding to a mellow groove.

The album opener and point of orientation is 'Haunts Of Ancient Peace', which formed as an idea when Morrison found a secondhand copy of Alfred Austin's 1902 book of that name. The phrase itself comes from 'The Palace Of Art' by Tennyson, who preceded Austin as poet laureate: 'And one, an English home ... a haunt of ancient peace'. Austin's prose is an exploration of Edwardian English identity, centred on a car journey through the countryside of the home counties and the characters' discussions of the national virtues to be found in village life mirrored in the landscape: including individualism and organicism. The quiet and gentle song celebrates in 'harmony and rhyme' the love and light to be found beside garden walls, where 'We see the new Jerusalem'. Building on the impression created by Isham's muted horn at the track's outset, Jef Labes added a celestial choir arrangement to convey the ethereal impression of ancestral voices in a hallowed place. Labes was a key influence on several Morrison albums, from *Moondance* to *Veedon Fleece*, and this was his last contribution until the 1986 album *No Guru, No Method, No Teacher*.

For most listeners, the highlight of *Common One* is 'Summertime In England', from which the album title is taken. Over 15 minutes long, it switches rhythm and speed and style, from funk to waltz, and is elevated by some of the most inspired and distinctive strings ever used on any

Morrison recording: arranged and conducted by Labes. Opening with Van Hooke's driving drum rhythm, swelling with Ellis' horn arrangement and pausing for John Allair's church organ solo, the song heads off at a new tempo for its second half, building to a new crescendo and fading to a stop, only to ask 'Can you feel the silence?'. The lyric started as a poem, and the references to writers – and particularly poets – reveal the origin in a narrative about Wordsworth and Coleridge heading from Somerset to the Lake District to work on poems that formed the core of their joint publication *Lyrical Ballads, with a Few Other Poems* (1798). Van is not here claiming literary kinship but a shared inspiration from the countryside: hence the song title. Judging by the emphasis on place, Morrison is imagining Avalon, but thinking about Wordsworth's 'Tintern Abbey', Eliot's 'East Coker', Blake's Albion, and Glastonbury Tor. Additionally, Van's obviously drawn to Ireland and the same association between land and literature suggested on *Veedon Fleece*, pointing towards the Celtic Renaissance a century after the English Romantics. 'Summertime In England' also celebrates the figure and idea of the common one – embodied in a red-robed walking companion with whom Morrison wants to listen to the silence and share the light of the summer sunset. We now know, too, that the line about 'your red robe dangling' dates back at least to Boston in 1968 when Morrison used it in the 'train' song he played with Payne and Kielbania. The image of the walking woman is reminiscent of Yeats' poem 'The Statesman's Holiday', in which each verse ends with 'Tall dames go walking in grass-green Avalon'. Morrison's own verdict on nature and love and spirit is simple and sublime – the same statement from *Astral Weeks*: to accept and not seek to ask why. His verdict on how pantheism feels, is personal, like hearing the gospel of Mahalia Jackson on the radio as a child.

'Satisfied' is a chugging funk with an insistent brass refrain and a solo that could've been recorded by American R&B band The Famous Flames. Any big band back in the day would've also recognised the call-and-response chant of the song title as Morrison bellows it out. It sounds like every one of the players shouts back, though only Hayes, Armstrong, Allair, and chief roadie Pete Brewis are credited as backing vocalists. The sentiment is similar to that found in the 1955 classic 'A Satisfied Mind' (the opening number on Dylan's own 1980 album *Saved*). Morrison's track expresses the feeling of being happy with one's world and of realising that to be satisfied, you have to look inside to challenge and change yourself before you can satiate spiritual hunger and thirst.

'Wild Honey' is the album's clearest love song, describing a communion linked to the excited rhythm of the heart. Like 'Country Fair', the title can be misleading – this is not a love song about an angel as sweet as 'Tupelo Honey', but a lyric about a loved one hearing the singer's passionate 'wild' heartbeat. It's also linked to the lovers' surroundings in nature. The light comes shining through, and Morrison feels the Spirit of Place – as D. H. Lawrence described it when attempting to give a name to the idea of a home(land) which he thought played a decisive role in forming a people's distinctive culture. For Morrison, the artist is singing, the band is gently playing, and the common connection with nature is felt in the music, which is 'tried and true'. Once more, he searches for the divine through music, with the idea of a 'common' oneness understood as a sublime unity: a Wordsworthian apprehension of a life force present in all natural objects. The song is bathed in Ellis' sweet horn arrangement, and Morrison's fondness for self-reference is again evident, linking this album's experimentation with *Astral Weeks*. In 'Wild Honey', we get words about being way up on the mountain and the hillside, which echoes 'Beside You', while the Sunday bells chime once more in 'Haunts Of Ancient Peace'.

'Spirit' is a song started during the making of *Into The Music* and is also the core of the loose concept of finding peaceful retreat in the countryside that's prevalent on *Common One*. It starts with a soft, almost spoken set of lines about lonely despair, against the band's sonic explorations; but, at the words 'Say, help me angel', the instruments burst loudly into life like a the musical accompaniment to a movie jump-scare. A song for the introverted, about a returning enthusiasm for life after dejection, it espouses a more defiant sentiment than the sadness of future Morrison songs, such as 'Melancholia' and 'Underlying Depression' on *Days Like This* (1995).

'When Heart is Open' returns the mood to the scene of 'Summertime In England' – venturing into the woods in an old greatcoat and walking boots, admiring his loved one, in tune with nature, and moving by the waterfall and across the meadow. The image of the deer is again used to suggest insight, revelation and self-knowledge. The song is as close to silence as music might get while remaining popular: a meditative soundscape of unfurling sound that suggests an opening flower.

The alternative take of 'When Heart Is Open' included on the 2008 remaster is an earlier recording with Toni Marcus playing violin and – importantly – sitar. Perhaps after the use of Hussain's tabla on *Into the*

Music, and the reference to karma on 'Satisfied', an overall debt to Indian music and philosophy is most clear on this version of 'When Heart Is Open'. There's greater attention to space, improvisation, the separation of instruments, and the elongation of single notes, with Morrison's vocal suitably altered. Though it's half the length of the album version, it settles into a beautiful lilting melody resting on Marcus' strings. The influence of jazz milestones like Miles Davis' *In a Silent Way* and John Coltrane's 'Psalm' from *A Love Supreme*, along with classical and ambient music, seems apparent on this recording.

Though there was some overdubbing in Sausalito, the album was mostly recorded in one intense nine-day period at the Super Bear Studios, housed in a former abbey in the village of Berre-les-Alpes in the French Alps, not far from Nice. The sequestered vibe added to the album's meditative feel and spectral qualities, as most of the band thought the place was haunted. Joni Mitchell's go-to producer Henry Lewy was engineer and co-producer. Though he had other recent stellar credentials, Lewy had worked with both Jackie DeShannon and Johnny Rivers back in the 1960s. Tour manager Mick Brigden arranged the trip to the south of France while management was still credited to Bill Graham, which would soon change. The cover shot taken by Rudolfo 'Rudi' Legname is in keeping with the album's dominant theme, and is based on a concept by Morrison, showing a figure in the distance that may be him striding up a country hillside.

Two outtakes made it onto *The Philosopher's Stone.* The old song 'Street Theory' is not a million miles from 'Satisfied', and swings along, driven by the brass and guitars. Intended as a slow song in keeping with the other tracks, 'Real Real Gone' was omitted from the album because it became too lively when Herbie Armstrong started to pick it up on his rhythm guitar. Morrison saved the song to re-record for *Enlightenment* in 1990, but Armstrong released his Morrison-produced version as a single in some regions.

Common One was not an easy sell in 1980. The six songs last almost an hour, and the two long tracks alone – 'Summertime In England' and 'When Heart Is Open' – are nearly as long as *A Period of Transition.* Warner Bros. issued a promo single of 'Summertime In England' b/w 'Haunts Of Ancient Peace' to little effect in the US, where *Common One* sold less than any 1970s Morrison album. In the UK, it became Morrison's lowest-placed album of the 1980s.

But the place to end the story of *Common One* is not in 1980, but almost 30 years later alongside *Astral Weeks*. Both albums met in 2009 with the release of *Astral Weeks: Live at the Hollywood Bowl*. Morrison concluded the album with a song called 'Common One'. He immediately invites the suffering 'common one' on a walk with him, and the lyric begins with the invitation from Austin's 'Haunts Of Ancient Peace' to go on a tour 'among the regions'. This is a journey through the beauty of the land, and a venture into the mystic church, which is the contemplative search for revelation inside the soul. Morrison references key starting points on his travels: the mystic church (of St. John) at Notting Hill Gate, the Swedenborgian New Church there, the nearby Westbourne Grove bus station, and the car journey to 'A Town Called Paradise': a song on Morrison's greatest 1980s album *No Guru, No Method, No Teacher*. He may have discovered Christian mystic Emmanuel Swedenborg via Blake (*The Marriage of Heaven and Hell* is a title Blake derived from Swedenborg). Swedenborg believed in a world of spiritual and physical correspondences, which chimes with Morrison's mystical perceptions. Indeed, the connections, synchronicities, and spiritual insights noted across Morrison's songs can increasingly be seen in terms of 'correspondences' – a Swedenborg term referring to the belief that every form in Heaven corresponds to one on Earth. Therefore, the idea of the 'common one' can probably be seen as all of the following: pantheism, a close walking companion, the red-robed Jesus come to Avalon, and divinity, as envisaged by Swedenborg whose writings promoted one universal church based on love and charity. Morrison also mentions the Brotherhood of Light – an ancient order pledged to protect the Holy Grail: bringing in the Arthurian legend integral to 'Summertime In England'.

Joining *Astral Weeks* and *Common One* in this way creates a circle around the 1970s, encompassing the key decade of Morrison's musical journey. They are his two most experimental and contemplative albums. Before and after the recording of *Common One*, he played small gigs in California, with at least 'Spirit' and 'Haunts Of Ancient Peace' appearing in the setlist before the record was made. In July, the band played at the Montreux-Detroit International Jazz festival. As we discussed earlier, this was a return after playing at Montreux in 1974, with both concerts released in 2006 on the *Live at Montreux* DVD set. In the mid-1970s, Morrison had played with a small scratch band put together by the festival founder Claude Nobs. Six years later, he had eight tried-and-tested musicians behind him: Allair and Labes on keyboards, Ellis and Isham in the brass section, Hayes on bass, John Platania on guitar, with Dahaud Shaar on drums and percussion alongside Peter Van Hooke. This was the backbone of the *Common One* studio band, without Cox and Armstrong but supplemented by returnees Shaar and Platania.

We can see on the video recording that before Morrison walks onstage to pick up his guitar, Labes cues up the band for the opener 'Wavelength', followed immediately by that other 1978 album stalwart 'Kingdom Hall'. Four still-unreleased *Common One* tracks pepper the set: 'Spirit', 'Satisfied', 'Haunts Of Ancient Peace', and 'Summertime In England'. With no strings, the brass section steals the show, particularly on the two *Into the Music* songs 'Troubadours' and the encore 'Angeliou'. After an opening chord, Isham starts 'Troubadours' with his piccolo trumpet. But it's Ellis who flies highest, and most of the musicians get their moments on other songs. Allair has an extended Hammond intro on 'Spirit', which Hayes really gets into, and by now it's clear the group are working tightly together. On a souped up, Latin-flavoured 'Moondance', Labes and Platania get to recreate their key parts from ten years earlier, and Platania takes a solo on an excellent version of 'Ballerina', showing exactly what it might've sounded like had Morrison recorded it at the end of the 1970s. Closing the show with the old favourites 'Wild Night', 'Listen To The Lion' and 'Tupelo Honey', brings the house down. The crowd demand one more song, and Morrison delivers the last of a string of fine vocal performances on 'Angeliou', ending a set lasting nearly 100 minutes. There's even time for a reinterpretation of 'Joyous Sound' and a reggae version of 'And It Stoned Me'.

After Montreux, three autumn gigs in the San Francisco area set a pattern for 1981, when Morrison only played two dates outside California. When his parents decided to move back to Belfast, he bought a new home in Mill Valley, Marin County. However, though he kept a foot in the US, he never thought himself properly at home in America and seeked to move back to England, buying a house in Stadhampton, Oxfordshire, and often living around Notting Hill. The romance with America took a long time to wane, but the number of US gigs declined from 1982, as the number in Europe increased. Morrison turned away from the west towards the north, reversing the journey sketched in 'Listen To The Lion'.

Though he was to make diverse and eclectic albums over the coming decades, Van forged a new sound in the 1980s, when the distinction between releases wouldn't always be as clear as in the 1970s: starting with the brace of records *Beautiful Vision* (1982) and *Inarticulate Speech of the Heart* (1983). The reference points now were not Kansas and Venice U.S.A. but Vanlose and Scandinavia. These would also be albums showing new personal and musical inspirations and a reduction in R&B influences in favour of jazz and Celtic rock, sometimes using Irish instruments; Morrison saying he felt it important for artists to engage with the music of their own culture.

Common One marked the end of an era of unpredictable musical investigation that had started with *Astral Weeks* and was another misunderstood record that underperformed commercially. But future releases were to find their market more easily. By the 1990s, Morrison's albums were entering the UK top 10, beginning with *Enlightenment*. But it took almost another 20 years to reach that position in the US when *Keep it Simple* – the album before *Astral Weeks: Live at the Hollywood Bowl* – hit number 10 on both sides of the Atlantic and reached similar positions across Europe. By this time, Morrison was a perennial figure in contemporary music. But his identity as a solo performer was forged in the 1970s – the extraordinary musical decade to which he made a unique contribution not only unlike that of any other artist but unlike anything that would follow.

Bibliography

Books

Bailie, S., *75 Van Songs: Into the Van Morrison Songbook* (Bloomfield, 2020)

Burke, D., *A Sense of Wonder: Van Morrison's Ireland* (Jawbone, 2013)

Buzzacott, M., Ford A., *Speaking in Tongues: The Songs of Van Morrison* (ABC Books, 2005)

Collis, J., *Van Morrison: Inarticulate Speech of the Heart* (Da Capo Press, 1997)

Dawe, G., *In Another World: Van Morrison and Belfast* (Merrion, 2020)

DeWitt, H, *Astral Weeks to Stardom 1968-72* (Horizon Books, 2020)

Hage, E., *The Words and Music of Van Morrison* (Greenwood, 2009)

Heylin, C., *Can You Feel the Silence? Van Morrison: A New Biography* (Penguin, 2004)

Hinton, B., *Celtic Crossroads: The Art of Van Morrison* (Sanctuary, 2000)

Hoskyns, B., *Small Town Talk: Bob Dylan, The Band, Van Morrison, Janis Joplin, Jimi Hendrix & Friends in the Wild Years of Woodstock* (Faber, 2017)

Marcus, G., *Listening to Van Morrison* (Faber, 2010)

Mills, P., *Hymns to the Silence: Inside the Words and Music of Van Morrison* (Continuum, 2010)

Morrison, V., *Lit Up Inside: Selected Lyrics* (Faber, 2014)

Morrison, V., *Keep 'Er Lit: New Selected Lyrics* (Faber, 2020)

Rogan, J., *Van Morrison: A Portrait of the Artist* (Proteus Books, 1984)

Rogan, J., *Van Morrison: No Surrender* (Secker & Warburg, 2005)

Turner, S., *Van Morrison: Too Late to Stop Now* (Bloomsbury, 1993)

Ultimate Music Guide: Van Morrison (Revised Edition) (Uncut, 2021)

Wrench, P., *Saint Dominic's Flashback: Van Morrison's Classic Album, Forty Years on* (Feedaread.com, 2012)

Yorke, R., *Van Morrison: Into the Music* (Futura, 1975)

Internet

http://www.vanmorrison.com
http://www.youtube.com/vanmorrison
https://www.oocities.org/tracybjazz/hayward/van-the-man.info/
http://ivan.vanomatic.de/home/home.shtml
http://mysticavenueblog.blogspot.com/
http://suncoastvanfans.blogspot.com/
https://borntolisten.com/van-morrison/
https://www.rocksbackpages.com/Library/Artist/van-morrison/